Cruising the Trent –Severn Canal, Georgian

Guides By Skipper Bob Pub

Planning Guides –
    Cruising Comfortably On a Budget. Tips on saving thousands of dollars while living and cruising on the coastal waters of the Eastern United States. How to outfit your boat and still be comfortable. ISBN 0-9662208-7-0 **$25**
    The Great Circle Route. Cruising the Great Circle Route up the East Coast, across the Great Lakes, down the Mississippi and Tenn-Tom Waterway to the Gulf Coast, and across the Gulf Coast to Florida. How to schedule the trip. ISBN 0-9662208-4-6 **$19**
    Bahamas Bound. A planning guide to the Bahamas. Who should consider going. What type of vessel. How to outfit your vessel for the Bahamas to save money and enjoy the trip. Marina prices and contact information. ISBN 0-9662208-9-7 **$16**

Cruising Guides –
    Anchorages Along The Intracoastal Waterway. Anchorages, free docks, bridge restrictions and waterway concerns from the Hudson River to Key West including the Okeechobee Waterway and St. Johns River. ISBN 0-9662208-3-8 **$17**
    Marinas Along The Intracoastal Waterway. Fuel prices, transient slip fees, courtesy cars, long-term slip fees, do-it-yourself yards, marina facilities, monthly rates, and haul out fees from the Hudson River to Key West. ISBN 0-9662208-0-3 **$15**
    Cruising the Gulf Coast. Cruising the Gulf Coast on the Gulf Intracoastal Waterway from Brownsville, TX to Flamingo, FL. Covers the waterway, anchorages, bridge and lock restrictions, marinas, and shopping along the way. ISBN 0-9727501-4-2 **$16**
    Cruising the New York Canal System. Depth and height restrictions. Lock locations and characteristics. Places to stay at no charge with water and electric. Includes the Erie, Oswego, Cayuga-Seneca, and Champlain Canals. ISBN 0-9662208-5-4 **$13**
    Cruising the Rideau and Richelieu Canals. How to plan a cruise of the historic waterways in Canada that include the Rideau Canal, Ottawa, St Lawrence River, Montreal, Quebec, Richelieu Canal, Chambly Canal, and Lake Champlain. ISBN 0-9662208-6-2 **$13**
    Cruising the Trent-Severn Canal, Georgian Bay and North Channel. Cruising the Trent-Severn Canal including fees, services available, where to stay, etc. Includes highlights of the Georgian Bay, North Channel and northern Lake Huron. ISBN 0-9662208-8-9 **$13**
    Cruising Lake Ontario. Information on harbors, anchorages, marinas, shopping, and local attractions. Distances to harbors with GPS coordinates at the entrance to each harbor. Includes the Thousand Islands and the Bay of Quinte. ISBN 0-9727501-0-X **$17**
    Cruising From Chicago to Mobile. Cruising the Inland River System from Chicago to Mobile, AL on Mobile Bay. Information on anchorages, free docks, marinas, bridge and lock restrictions, and navigational concerns for this route. ISBN 0-9727501-5-0 **$16**
    Cruising Lake Michigan. Information on ports and harbors, approach GPS waypoints, anchorages, Lake Michigan precautions, marinas, shopping, and local attractions. Includes Green and Grand Traverse Bays. ISBN 0-9727501-5-0 **$19**

Nautical Reading –
    Seven Miles an Hour. Witty, but to the point. This book gives the reader the basic concept of what you will go through when deciding to buy a boat and live aboard. Excellent read for anyone interested in boating. ISBN 0-9727501-6-9 **$23**

Cruising the Trent –Severn Canal, Georgian Bay and North Channel

Ordering Skipper Bob Publications

AGLCA – 500 Oakbrook Lane, Summerville, SC 29485.
    Phone 877-478-5667. Internet – www.greatloop.org.

Bluewater Books & Charts - 1811 Cordova Road, Fort Lauderdale, FL 33316.
    Phone 954-763-6533. Internet - www.bluewaterweb.com.

Defender Industries – 42 Great Neck Road, Waterford, CT 06385
    Phone 800-628-8225. Internet – www.defender.com.

Landfall Navigation® – 151 Harvard Avenue, Stamford, CT 06902
    Phone 800-941-2219. Internet - www.landfallnavigation.com/**skipperbob**.html.

Sonset Marine – 3732 Bailey Road, Marlette, MI 48453.
    Phone 989-635-2696. Internet – www.sonsetmarine.com.

The Nautical Mind – 249 Queen's Quay West, Toronto, Ontario, Canada M5J 2N5
    Phone 800-463-9951. Internet - www.nauticalmind.com.

Watermark Publishing – PO Box 67, Elon, NC 27244-0067.
    Phone 800-803-0809. Internet -www.cruisingguide.com

Where you can pick up Skipper Bob Publications

AL: Dog River Marina, 5004 Dauphine Island Parkway, Mobile, AL 36605, Ph 251-471-5449
FL: First Mates Ship Store, 235 Yacht Club Drive, St Augustine, FL 32905, Ph 904-829-0184
    Marathon Discount Books, 2219 Overseas Hwy, Marathon, FL 33050, Ph 305-289-2066
    Municipal Marina, 111A Avenida Menedez, St Augustine, FL 32048, Ph 904-824-9300
    Pier 17 Marine, Inc., 4619 Roosevelt Blvd., Jacksonville, FL 32210, Ph 904-387-4669
    Sailorman, 350E State Road 84, Ft Lauderdale, FL 33316, Ph 954-522-6716
    Sailors Exchange, 222 W King Street, St Augustine, FL 32085, Ph 904-808-0667
    St. Petersburg Municipal Marina, 500 1st Ave SE, St. Petersburg, FL 33701, Ph 727-823-2555
    Sunset Marina Key West, 5555 College Road, Key West, FL 33040, Ph 305-296-7101
    Titusville Municipal Marina, 451 Marina Road, Titusville, FL 32796, Ph 321-383-5600
    West Marine, 1875 N. US Highway 1, Fort Pierce, FL 34946, Ph 772-460-9044
    West Marine, 12189 US Highway 1, North Palm Beach, FL 33408, Ph 561-775-1434
    Yacht Basin Ships Store, 1306 Lee Street, Fort Myers, FL, Ph 239-334-6446
GA: Hattie's Books, 1531 Newcastle St., Brunswick, GA 31520, Ph 912-554-8677
    Thunderbolt Marine, PO Box 5628, Savannah, GA 31414, Ph 912-356-3875
KY: Green Turtle Bay Resort & Marina, PO Box 102, Grand Rivers, KY 42045,
    Ph 270-362- 8364
MD: Fawcett Boat Supplies, 110 Compromise Street, Annapolis, MD 21401, Ph 800-456-9151
    Spring Cove Marina, PO Box 160, Solomons, MD 20688, Ph 410-326-2161

Cruising the Trent –Severn Canal, Georgian Bay and North Channel

NC: **Alligator River Marina,** PO Box 719, Columbia, NC 27925, Ph 252796-0333
Coinjock Marina, 321 Waterlily Road, Coinjock, NC 27923, Ph 252-453-3271
Dowry Creek Marina, 110 Spinnaker Run Road, Belhaven, NC, Ph 252-943-2728
Page after Page Bookstore, 111 South Water Street, Elizabeth City, NC, Ph 252-335- 7243
Scuttlebutt, 433 Front Street, Beaufort, NC 28516, Ph 252-728-7765
NJ: **Utsch's Marina,** 1121 Route 109, Cape May, NJ 08204, Ph 609-884-2051
NY: **Ess Kay Yards, Inc,** 5307 Guy Young Road, Brewerton, NY 13029, Ph 315-676-2711
New York Nautical, 140 West Broadway, NY, NY 10013, Ph 212-962-4522
Oswego Marina, 3 Basin Street, Oswego, NY 13126, Ph 315-342-0436
Rondout Yacht Basin, PO Box 257, Connelly, NY 12417, Ph 845-331-7061
Troy Town Dock and Marina, 427 River Street, Troy, NY 12180, Ph 518-272-5341
Waterford Canal Center, One Tug Boat Alley, Waterford, NY 12188, Ph 518-527-5041
Winter Harbor Marina, PO Box 630, Brewerton, NY 13029, Ph 315-676-9276
PA: **Pilothouse Nautical Books,** 1600 S Delaware Ave, Philadelphia, PA, Ph 215-336-6414
RI: **Armchair Sailor Bookstore,** 543 Thames Street, Newport, RI 02840, Ph 800-292-4278
SC: **Downtown Marina,** 1006 Bay Street, Beaufort, SC 29902, Ph 843-524-4422
Harborwalk Books, 723 Front Street, Georgetown, SC 29440, Ph 843-546-8212
JJW Luden & Co, 78 Alexander Street, Charleston, SC 29401, Ph 843-723-7829
Osprey Marina, 8400 Osprey Road, Myrtle Beach, SC 29588, Ph 843-215-5353
Port Royal Landing Marina, 1 Landing Drive, Port Royal, SC, 29935, Ph 843-525-6664
VA: **Dozier's Regatta Point,** 137 Neptune Lane, Deltaville, VA 23043, Ph 804-776-6711
Nauti Nell's, PO Box 515, Deltaville, VA 23043, Ph 804-776-9811
WT Brownley Co, 226 E Main Street, Norfolk, VA 23510, Ph 757-622-7589

NOTE: If you are not able to locate the Skipper Bob Book that you desire, contact Skipper Bob Publications, PO Box 1125, Deltaville, VA 23043, Ph 804-776-8899 or email SkipperBob@att.net.

Cruising the Trent –Severn Canal, Georgian Bay and North Channel

WINTER HARBOR L.L.C.
FULL SERVICE BOATYARD GUARANTEED STRUCTURAL REPAIRS
FAMILY OWNED AND OPERATED

WINTER HARBOR L.L.C. COME VISIT OUR STATE OF THE ART, FULL SERVICE MARINA. LOCATED ON THE ONEIDA RIVER IN BREWERTON, NY 1 MILE WEST OF ONEIDA LAKE.
- ACCOMMODATIONS FOR VESSELS TO 150 FEET
- COMPLIMENTARY COURTESY VEHICLE
- 24 HR. HIGH SPEED PAY AT PUMP FUELING
- DOCKSIDE WATER & CABLE TV
- ON SITE COMPUTER PORT AVAILABLE
- PRISTINE BATHROOMS & SHOWERS
- 110/220 ELECTRIC SERVICE 30 & 50 AMP
- PUMP OUT SERVICE
- 70 TON MARINE TRAVEL LIFT
- 27,000 LB. MARINE TRAVEL FORK TRUCK
- 46,000 SQ. FT. OF **INDOOR HEATED WINTER STORAGE!**
- 12 MINUTES TO SYRACUSE INTERNATIONAL AIRPORT AND MAJOR SHOPPING MALLS

BOAT/U.S. DISCOUNTS!
25% OFF TRANSIENT DOCKAGE & MORE!

QUALITY WORKMANSHIP

OUR TEAM HAS OVER 20 YRS EXPERIENCE IN MARINE REPAIRS, MAINTENANCE AND CUSTOM FABRICATING.
WINTER HARBOR OFFERS A FULL LINE OF SERVICES INCLUDING:
- BOTTOM PAINTING
- FIBERGLASS AND GEL-COAT REPAIR
- BUFF & WAX SERVICE
- ENGINE REPAIR & MAINTENANCE
- PROPELLER, SHAFT & HULL REPAIR
- ELECTRONIC & CANVAS REPAIR
- BOW THRUSTER INSTALLATION
- ALSO WE CAN CUSTOM DESIGN AND CREATE ALL YOUR FABRICATING NEEDS

TREAT YOURSELF AND YOUR CREW TO THE CLEANEST AND NEWEST FACILITY WEST OF NYC!

MAIL
P.O. BOX 630
BREWERTON, NY 13029

315-676-WARM (9276)
315-668-9229 FAX
www.winterharborllc.com

Cruising the Trent-Severn Waterway, Georgian Bay and North Channel.

Table of Contents

Chapter 1 - Introduction	6
Begin at the Beginning	6
Customs	7
Provisions	9
Cash, Checks and Credit Cards	9
Holding Tank	10
Electrical	10
Fishing	10
Pets	10
Weapons	11
Radio License	11
Navigation	11
Contributors	11
Arrival in Canada	12
Trenton	12
Chapter 2 – Trent-Severn Canal History	14
Chapter 3 – The Trent-Severn Waterway	17
Waterway Fees	19
Chapter 4 – Trenton to Rice Lake	22
Chapter 5 – Ontonabee River and Rice Lake	29
Chapter 6 – Kawartha Lakes	34
Chapter 7 – The Talbot River	39
Chapter 8 – The Severn River	45
Chapter 9 – The Georgian Bay	50
Weather	50
Charts	51
Chapter 10 – The North Channel	63
Chapter 11 – Northern Lake Huron	71
Les Cheneaux Islands	72
Saint Ignace	73
Mackinac Island	73
Mackinaw City	74
Bois Blanc Island	75
Cheboygan	75
Appendix 1 – Charts and Reference Books	77
Appendix 2 – Hours of Operation & Fees	78
Appendix 3 – Contributors	79
Index	80

Cruising the Trent-Severn Waterway, Georgian Bay and North Channel.

Chapter 1
Introduction

The northwest corner of Ontario Providence in Canada offers some of the most beautiful cruising grounds in North America. From the Trent-Severn Waterway to the North Channel and through Georgian Bay you experience a wide variety of cruising characteristics sure to please the most discriminating boater. This area makes a great place to spend the summer with its warm days, cool nights, fresh water and friendly people. Whether you are just spending the summer or traveling through on the Great Loop Route, you are sure to treasure your memories of this area.

The Trent-Severn Waterway is 240 statute miles long and runs roughly west from Trenton on Lake Ontario to Port Severn on the Georgian Bay. The Georgian Bay lies in the northeast corner of Lake Huron and the North Channel occupies the northern most part of Lake Huron.

The Georgian Bay lies basically northeast and is 168.5 statute miles long via the small craft channel. The small craft channel (which can easily handle 50 foot boats) starts at Port Severn in the eastern most edge of the Georgian Bay and follows the northern shoreline around the upper end of Georgian Bay to Killarney.

The North Channel lies roughly east/west and is 138 statute miles long by the protected route. It starts at Killarney and lies along the northern most shore to Thessalon and then southwest to De Tour Village.

For the entire trip from Trenton on Lake Ontario to De Tour Village on Lake Huron your vessel will be in very protected waters. Only during the last 40 miles do you come out from behind islands and cross the open end of the North Channel. If you pick a good day to cross Lake Simcoe on the Trent-Severn Waterway and the last 40 miles of the North Channel you should have a very enjoyable and safe voyage.

Begin at the Beginning

Information on the Trent-Severn Waterway can be obtained from many websites. Two very good ones are;

Parks Canada – http://www.pc.gc.ca/lhn-nhs/on/trentsevern/index, 888-773-8888 (US only) and 705-750-4900 (Canada).

About TrentSevern.com – http://www.trentsevern.com/info.

Cruising The Trent-Severn Waterway, Georgian Bay, And North Channel
Chapter 1 - Introduction

Information on customs and other procedures for entering Canada may be obtained from the Canada Border Services Agency website http://cbsa-asfc.gc.ca. Click on Travelers and then go to Visitors to Canada.

A good source for information on boating in Canada can be found at Pat's Boating in Canada http://boating/ncf.ca/ . Information on crossing Lake Ontario and cruising the Bay of Quinte can be found in our publication *Cruising Lake Ontario.*

Before you start for Canada be sure to get your charts. Access to shopping where you can buy charts is somewhat limited. In addition, proper planning will make your journey more enjoyable. A complete list of charts and other cruising resources is provided in Appendix 1. As you go through this book, we will refer to the charts by number so you can easily plot your progress and destination.

Customs
Entering Canada

Canadian law requires that all persons entering Canada must carry proof of citizenship and identity. Visit http://www.cbsa.gc.ca for details.

Vessels traveling from the U.S. must proceed directly to the nearest designated telephone reporting marine site. The captain of the vessel must report to the Canada Border Services Agency by calling 1-888-226-7277. It is important to note that no one except the captain may leave the vessel until authorized to do so by the CBSA. You will be presented with a report number that you should record in the event you are requested to provide this number later on by a border services officer. To get a list of the designated telephone reporting marine sites, call 1-888-226-7277 prior to entering Canada.

When reporting to the CBSA be prepared to provide the following information:

- The location of the vessel.
- Vessel registration/documentation number (have papers on board).
- Final destination in Canada.
- The names, dates of birth, citizenships and countries of residence of all passengers.
- Purpose of trip to Canada.
- Length of absence from Canada for Canadian citizens.
- Customs declaration for each person on board.

All persons must declare any personal goods they are importing, including firearms and weapons and report all currency and monetary instruments exceeding $10,000 (Canadian).

Returning to the United States

U.S. law requires that Americans entering the U.S. from Canada by air must have a valid passport. This requirement will be extended to sea and land travel by the Summer of 2008.

All pleasure craft must report immediately after arriving in the United States to U.S. Customs at a port of entry.

One exception to the requirement to report immediately to Customs at a port of entry is the Canadian Border Boat Landing (I-68) program. Form I-68 permits a boater to make subsequent recreation entries into the United States without the need for additional inspections for the

Cruising The Trent-Severn Waterway, Georgian Bay and North Channel
Chapter 1 - Introduction

balance of the boating season. The initial inspection involves an interview, checking the individual in the Interagency Border Inspection System and other law enforcement databases, processing three photographs, imprinting a single fingerprint on each copy of the form and payment of the fee. Additional details on the program may be found by visiting www.cbp.gov.

For inspection at a port of entry a boater may utilize one of the 33 Outlying Area Reporting Stations (OARS) videophones for admission to the United States. OARS costs nothing but requires the boater to check into a port each time when returning to the U.S. The system is comprised of an AutoDial telephone, a video transceiver, a monitor, a facial camera and a document camera. Videophones installed at public marinas along the Canadian border provide an automated inspection service enabling two-way visual and audio communication between the inspector and the applicant.

Joint Canadian and United States Programs

The following are joint inspection programs which allow pre-screened, low-risk travelers to be processed with little or no delay by United States and Canadian border officials.

CANPASS Private Boat Program
The CANPASS Private Boat Program is a result of the Canada-United States Accord on Our Shared Border. If you often enter Canada from the United States using a private pleasure craft, a membership in the CANPASS Private Boat Program may enable you to pass through customs more quickly. There is a non-refundable five year processing fee of $40 Canadian for each person over 18 years of age. For more information contact CCRA at 888-226-7277 or visit www.cbsa.gc.ca.

NEXUS
Similar to Canada's CANPASS program, the NEXUS alternative inspection program is a membership program. Approved applicants are issued a photo-identification/proximity card. NEXUS members have the benefit of expedited processing in both marine and highway modes. Recreational boaters may report their arrival with just a phone call to U.S. Customs and Border Protection and can use their NEXUS membership in lieu of Form I-68 for reporting purposes. The cost is $50 U.S. or $80 Canadian for a five year period. For further information contact 866-639-8726 or visit www.cbp.gov.

Don't forget flag courtesy. You should hoist the yellow quarantine flag when you enter Canadian waters and display this flag until after you have cleared customs. Once you have received your customs clearance, enter the customs clearance number in your log. Then lower the yellow quarantine flag and raise the Canadian Courtesy Flag. Display this courtesy flag until you depart Canadian waters.

User Fee Decal

If the vessel is 30 feet or longer, the owner must obtain a user fee decal when entering the U.S., available for $25 at the U.S. Customs and Border Protection office. This decal must be affixed near a vessel's main boarding area. This number will be requested when the vessel

Cruising The Trent-Severn Waterway, Georgian Bay and North Channel
Chapter 1 - Introduction

reports to customs. Applications may be made by visiting http:// CBP.gov and clicking on "Travel". Info may also be obtained by calling 317-298-1245.

Provisions

Before leaving the U.S. you do not need to stock up on provisions. With the currency rate of exchange at publication (March 2008) at par, buying food in Canada is about the same as in the US. In addition, Canada has restrictions and limits on the amount certain food stuffs you are allowed to import. Alcohol and tobacco products are heavily taxed so you may want to import the maximum allowed.

Each adult is allowed to import *only one* of the following amounts of alcohol free of duty and taxes.
- 1.5 liters of wine.
- 1.14 liters of liquor.
- A total of 1.14 liters of wine and liquor.
- 24 (12 oz) cans or bottles of beer

Note that the minimum age for possession and consumption of alcohol in Canada is 18 or 19 years of age depending on the province or territory. Also, "cooler" products such as wine and beer coolers are classified according to the alcoholic beverage they contain, so long as it is greater than 0.5% by volume.

You are allowed to import all of the following amounts of tobacco without paying duty:

- 200 cigarettes.
- 50 cigars or cigarillos.
- 200 grams (7 oz) of manufactured tobacco.
- 200 tobacco sticks.

Cash, Checks and Credit Cards

Access to cash is not a problem in Canada. Most large stores and marinas take credit cards. Access to money machines (ATM) is easy in many places along the waterway. ATM machines will issue you Canadian Money and convert the cost to US dollars and debit your bank account giving you the most favorable rate of exchange. Just like going into a bank. However as you get further up the Trent-Severn you may find it harder to find banks and/or money machines. Exchange rates vary from bank to bank and it may be to your advantage to use credit cards whenever possible. Most merchants will accept U.S. dollars, however, you most likely will not receive the going rate of exchange. If you have access to the Internet, the web site www.oanda.com/convert/cheatsheet provides real time conversion rates for either US or Canadian money.

Don't change too much money to Canadian dollars. Try to estimate your requirements before hand. You will lose a little on the exchange if you have to change your Canadian Dollars back to US at the end of the trip.

Banks at either end do not convert coins. So when arriving in Canada put all your US coins in a drawer and forget them until you return to the US. When getting ready to return to the US try to spend all your Canadian coins and keep only paper bills to exchange back.

Cruising The Trent-Severn Waterway, Georgian Bay and North Channel
Chapter 1 - Introduction

Most stores will not take personal checks in US dollars.

Tax Rebates

Visitors to Canada at one time were able to apply for a refund of GST paid on certain items. This program was eliminated in August 2007.

Holding Tank

While in Canada you will need to use your holding tank and pump out at marinas. Make sure your vessel is equipped with a reliable holding tank and that you are not discharging directly overboard. Provisions for overboard discharge (Y valve) when in international waters (the ocean) should be locked in the holding tank position. Direct discharge of gray water is acceptable in all waters described in this book.

The MSD III (Marine Sanitation Device) is a holding tank and is permitted in all Canadian and US waters. The MSD I, like Electro San® is not legal in the waters of Ontario and Lake Michigan.

Electrical

Many of the marinas do not have 50A service. In some cases you can make 50A with a twin male 30A to 50A female adapter (Reverse Y Adapter Marco 167RY). In addition, if you have a 50A male plug, but can get by on 30A (not 240V or two phase), you should also carry a male 30A to female 50A adapter (Marco Adapter 117A).

Some of the canal stops do not have 30A, but do have either 15A or 20A. Vessels requiring 30A that can operate on reduced current (shut off air conditioner, water heater, etc.) should carry both the 15A male to 30A female adapter (Marco adapter 83A) and 20A male to 30A female adapter (Marco adapter 84A).

One oddity that we have noted concerns some 30A receptacles we encountered in the Canadian Park System. Although they are 30 amp receptacles we found some that were on breakers of only 20 or even 15 amps. The receptacle configuration was a convenience to assist boaters in plugging in, but did not provide the 30 amp power implied by the receptacle.

Fishing

For those boaters who like to fish, Canada provides great opportunities. Regulations relative to licenses, catch limits, etc. vary by Province just as in the United States. Penalties for fishing without a valid license can be substantial so do your homework and obtain the proper documents.

Pets

Pet dogs and cats may enter Canada if accompanied by a valid rabies vaccination certificate issued by a licensed veterinarian that clearly identifies the pet and shows that they are currently vaccinated against rabies. This certificate must identify the animal's breed, color, weight, plus

Cruising The Trent-Severn Waterway, Georgian Bay and North Channel
Chapter 1 - Introduction

indicate the name of the licensed rabies vaccine used (trade name), serial number and duration of validity. Pet dogs and cats under three months in age do not require documentation.

Firearms and Weapons

Canada has very strict firearms and weapons laws and before you attempt to take these items into Canada it is imperative that you contact the Canada Firearms Centre (1-800-731-4000, www.cafc.gc.ca) prior to your entry for information about what is permitted and how to apply for the proper permits. In general:

- You must be at least 18 years of age.
- You can import non-restricted and restricted firearms, provided you meet all the requirements.
- You cannot import prohibited firearms, weapons or devices, including silencers, replica firearms, switchblades and other weapons.
- You cannot import mace or pepper spray.

You must declare all weapons and firearms at the CBSA port of entry or they will be seized and you may be subject to arrest.

Radio License

As most boaters know, the Federal Communications Commission (FCC) dropped the requirement for each boater to have a valid FCC license on their vessel if they had an operating VHF radio, SSB, or other RF transmitting device. In April 1999, Canada also dropped the requirement for a FCC license for the VHF radio. However, Canada does have a requirement for each operator of a VHF radio to have a Restricted Radiotelephone Operator's Certificate (ROC). The sole examiner for the ROC is the Canadian Power & Sail Squadrons (CPS). To legally use your VHF radio in Canada you are required to have the ROC. Contact the CPS at 1-416-293-2438 or toll free in Canada at 1-888-277-2628 for information on the Study Guide for the Restricted Operator's Certificate (RIC-23), inexpensive classroom course or to take the exam. A current FCC liscense is accepted as a substitute for the ROC.

Navigation

An important note. **This book should NOT be used for navigation**. The most recent changes to the waterway cannot and will not be included in this book. The prudent cruiser will rely on the proper charts, navigation equipment and latest notices to mariners for all navigation information.

Contributors

One final note. We encourage you to send us comments about this book. Whether they are about your likes or dislikes, navigational or other updates, we want them. Email to skipperbob@att.net. Each will be carefully reviewed and when appropriate will be used in the

Cruising The Trent-Severn Waterway, Georgian Bay and North Channel
Chapter 1 - Introduction

annual update. Navigational updates will be posted on the Skipper Bob website until incorporated into the next edition. A list of current contributors may be found in Appendix 3.

Arrival in Canada

If you have not yet cleared Canadian Customs, Trenton is the place to do it. Hoist your yellow quarantine flag when you enter Canadian waters and leave it displayed on landing in Trenton. See the approach in our book *Cruising Lake Ontario.*

Whether you are coming from the west via the Murray Canal or the east from Kingston, you will reach the Bay of Quinte. Follow your chart (2021, sheet 2 of 4) and enter the Trent River at Trenton. Just inside the mouth of the river on the west bank before the first fixed bridge is the Fraser Park Marina (Trenton Marina) (613-394-2561,G,D,P). This is a good place to stop to clear customs, change money and stock provisions. Within a five minute walk are restaurants, banks, a pharmacy, several grocery stores, a marine store, a laundry, the post office and a liquor store. Two supermarkets are approximately a mile away. Across the river on the east bank is a large marina enclosed in a basin. This is part of the Fraser Park Marina and does not cater to transient vessels. If you want a marina in Trenton you must use the one on the west bank just before the bridge.

A quiet anchorage with good holding ground is available just above the second bridge between red buoys "T2" and "T4" to starboard.

Only the captain may depart the vessel before you have cleared customs. Nothing should be removed or taken aboard until after you have cleared customs. Go to the phone in the marina parking lot and call customs at 1-888-226-7277. Follow the procedures outlined previously in this chapter. When the process is completed the customs officer will give you a clearance number. Go back to your vessel and record the number in your log. Remove the yellow quarantine flag and hoist the Canadian Courtesy flag. You should fly the Canadian Courtesy flag during your entire stay in Canadian waters and only remove it at the end of the trip as you approach US waters. Then you again will raise the yellow quarantine flag until clearing customs.

Now that you are in Canada there are some things that should be done before you begin your trip through the Trent-Severn Waterway. Go to a bank and change your money. There are several banks in Trenton within 3 blocks of the marina.

Throughout this book we will identify marinas that accept transient vessels, whether they offer gas (G) and/or diesel (D), provide pump out (P) and offer WiFi. We also will not normally list transient rates, however, expect to pay between $1.00 to $1.75/foot. Most marinas in Canada respond to VHF Channel 68. Do not call them on VHF Channel 16.

Trenton

Trenton is an excellent place to spend a couple of days taking on provisions and enjoying the local tourist scene. The street that crosses the first bridge on the Trenton River (The Gateway to the Trent Bridge) is Dundas Street (Highway 2). West along Dundas Street you will find several restaurants, pizzerias, banks, gift shops and finally a movie theater, 24 hour A&P (supermarket) and a used book store across the street. To the east across the bridge you will find a Price Chopper (supermarket) and two blocks further an Arbys and several small shops and fast food restaurants. Finally north five blocks on the west bank of the Trent-Severn River is a KFC.

Cruising The Trent-Severn Waterway, Georgian Bay and North Channel
Chapter 1 - Introduction

The Visitor Center is on the west bank located three blocks north on Front Street on the right side. At the Visitor Center you can obtain local maps and pamphlets about sites to visit in the area.

If you are interested in fishing while in Canada, now would be a good time to check out the rules and regulations. Check with the Visitor Center or marina to find out where you go to get your fishing license. Along the Trent-Severn Canal you can catch rock bass, yellow perch, large and small mouth bass, muskellunge, northern pike, lake trout, and the most famous of all, walleye.

Fraser Park features several walking and biking trails, Friday night concerts featuring local musicans, and a Farmers Market every Thursday and Saturday morning. And Mount Pelion features an observation deck that provides a panoramic view of the waterway including the first lock on the Trent-Severn.

Beer and alcohol are not sold in regular stores in Canada. They are only sold at controlled establishments. Beer is sold at "The Beer Store". You won't have any trouble recognizing The Beer Store. It is painted a bright orange color. In Trenton The Beer Store is across the Trent River 5 blocks. Follow Dundas Street east and turn left on Byron Street. It is immediately on the right. Alcohol is sold at Liquor Control Board of Ontario outlets (LCBO). The large LCBO sign is hard to miss. In Trenton the LCBO is 3 blocks north on Front Street. Turn left on Ford Street and it is immediately on your right. As you go through this book, I will identify those LCBO and Beer Store outlets within easy walk on the Trent-Severn Canal.

Most vessels arriving at the Trent-Severn Canal will have already stepped their mast if needed to clear the 22' bridges. If not, the Bay of Quinte Yacht Club in Belleville (9 miles east of Trenton on north shore) or the CFB Trenton Yacht Club in Trenton (3 miles east of Trenton north of Baker Island) provide a crane for a fee for do-it-yourself boaters to lower their mast.

Cruising The Trent-Severn Waterway, Georgian Bay, And North Channel

Chapter 2
Trent-Severn Canal History

Unlike the Trent-Severn, the Erie Canal began with a purpose. A plan was made and after much effort the Erie Canal was completed in only 8 years. Such is not the history of the Trent-Severn Waterway. From beginning to end would require nearly 90 years spurred on by military, economical and political forces.

As early as 1780 the Canadians started to look for a good route to transport men and supplies from the northern region of Canada to the southern border that was free of possible military intervention by Americans. In our early history as neighbors, the Canadians and American forces eyed each other with suspicion. For many years some in power felt we would go to war. After all, the history of European countries indicated that rarely did neighboring countries avoid conflict for too long. By 1815 the Trent-Severn route had been ruled out as a military necessity and "dropped from the drawing boards".

By the early 1800s men were moving supplies and goods freely about lower Canada using boats and portages on the many fresh water lakes in what is now southwest Ontario. Planning began again around 1825 to build a canal to move goods and materials from the Georgian Bay to Lake Ontario via water. However, after much thought it was realized that although that route would be shorter, it had two distinct disadvantages. First, vessels would have to be smaller than those used on the Great Lakes. Large vessels would have to be unloaded and reloaded at both ends. Secondly, the numerous locks would slow down the movement of goods such that any time advantage of the shorter route would be lost. The Trent-Severn Canal fell by the wayside again.

Dreams die hard. Forces in and out of the government continued to push for a canal from Port Severn to Trenton. In 1833 a grant was made for the construction of a lock at Bobcaygeon. James Bethune began construction of the first lock on the Trent-Severn in 1833. It was to be made of wood and sped up the transportation between Sturgeon and Pigeon Lakes. The plans called for a lock 120 feet long, and 28 feet wide with a lift of 10 feet. By 1834 the lock was finished as well as the entrance and exit canals. However, when water was let into the system it was a disaster. The lock had been built at the wrong level and on porous rock. The water entering the upper side of the lock literally disappeared into the ground before ever reaching the lock.

Steamboats picking up wood

Virtually abandoned for a period, an effort was made in 1836 to repair the design flaws and get the wooden lock at Bobcaygeon working. After two years and much money, the improved and upgraded wooden lock was put into service in 1838. However, because it was built at the wrong elevation, it did not provide the desired water depth within the lock and was not long enough for the only large vessel on the lake at that time. So this wooden lock at Bobcaygeon was only used for small boats and floating logs until 1855. At that time a contract was let to again improve and upgrade the Bobcaygeon lock and by 1857 a new limestone masonry lock 134 feet long and 33 feet wide was in place. This lock remained in service until 1921 when the new concrete lock replaced it.

In the meantime, numerous projects were undertaken between 1834 and 1920 to improve movement of goods, raw material and people in and around the lakes in southwest Ontario. Some dams were built to raise water levels to make some lakes more navigable. Waterslides were built around rapids to aid in moving timber from one level to another. A few locks were built to improve movement between lakes, such as one at Hastings. Then in the middle 1800s steamboats became more numerous and more pressure was brought to bear to add more locks.

In the late 1800s trains expanded throughout the area to carry out lumber, bring in finished goods and transport tourists. The trains only seemed to emphasize that there was no need for a Trent-Severn Canal. The trains would provide the needed transportation. However, the trains could not access all areas of the lakes and as business increased more steamboats were added and more pressure applied to add locks between lakes.

By 1875 the Canadian Government took the position that the locks were needed only for interlake transportation and the government would not support a complete system. That being said, more locks were built connecting still more lakes. Young's Point lock in 1870, Fenelon Falls lock in 1882, and Burleigh Falls in 1887, just to mention a few.

Peterborough Lock under construction - 1902

From 1896 to 1904 the government expanded the lock system to include five locks from Peterborough to Lakefield. The most impressive lock to that time was the 65-foot high Peterborough Lift Lock completed in 1904.

In 1907 a new player entered the scene. Hydroelectric power! Almost overnight politicians realized that controlling the rivers and dams between the lakes in this region represented a goldmine. By letting contracts to build hydroelectric dams with locks, the government could obtain money to build the locks and dams, pay for annual upkeep, provide the nation with cheap power and provide an efficient waterway. From then on the Trent-Severn Canal never looked back.

From 1907 to 1918 the Trent River was developed with locks and power generating dams. By 1918 there was a complete water route from Trenton on Lake Ontario to Lake Couchiching, 90% of the way to the Georgian Bay.

From 1913 to 1917 the push was on to complete the final 10%. The lock at Port Severn was added first and then Swift Rapids and Couchiching. Now all that remained was the lock at Big Chute. To speed up the progress of the canal it was decided in 1917 to build a temporary marine railway at Big Chute while the lock was constructed. The marine railway went into operation in July 1918. Meanwhile construction on the lock and dam at Big Chute began. World War I was

Cruising The Trent-Seven Waterway, Georgian Bay, and North Channel
Chapter 2 – Trent – Severn History

winding down. Funds became tight. In 1920 funds ran out and construction on the two locks and canal at Big/Little Chute stopped. They would never resume. Instead, in 1923 the marine railway at Big Chute was enlarged to handle larger vessels.

After several delays, the last two mile long canal was completed in June 1920. This canal between Lake Couchiching and the Severn River completed the water route between Port Severn and Trenton. The official opening of the canal came on July 6, 1920 at 1:30PM. Only a few people were present. Simultaneously the motor launch Irene left Trenton headed for Port Severn. On July 20, 1920 Irene arrived in Port Severn becoming the first vessel to complete the trip.

It had taken more than 90 years. The cost exceeded $19 million dollars. Today this marvelous waterway provides for wonderful boating, is a great tourist attraction, and generates electric power. Over the years some of the locks and dams have been rebuilt and modernized, but for the most part the canal still consists of locks and dams built more than 75 years ago that are operated manually.

For additional reading, *A Work Unfinished* by James Angus, is excellent. This book contains a much more detailed history and many wonderful old photographs of actual lock and dam construction. The book sells for $28.00 (Canadian) in many gift shops and bookstores along the canal. The book ISBN number is 0-9694197-3-2 and it can be ordered by contacting Severn Publications Limited, 95 Matchedash Street N, #404, Orillia, Ontario L3V 4T9, phone 705-329-2127 or E-mail jangus@bconnex.net.

For now, let's get back to today and in the next chapter start our journey through the Trent-Severn Waterway.

Cruising The Trent Severn Waterway, Georgian Bay, And North Channel

Chapter 3
The Trent-Severn Waterway

The Trent-Severn Waterway starts at Trenton, which is 243 feet above sea level. For the first 35 locks you will be locking up and eventually reach the high water point at Balsam Lake at 840 feet above sea level. From that point on it is a steady decline as you work your way to Port Severn and 576 feet above sea level. The Trent-Severn Waterway is actually the correct name for the waterway between Trenton and Port Severn and is made up by a number of canals and locks connecting lakes and rivers. However, you will hear the expression "The Trent-Severn Canal" much more frequently than "The Trent-Severn Waterway". For purposes of this book, we will use the two expressions interchangeably.

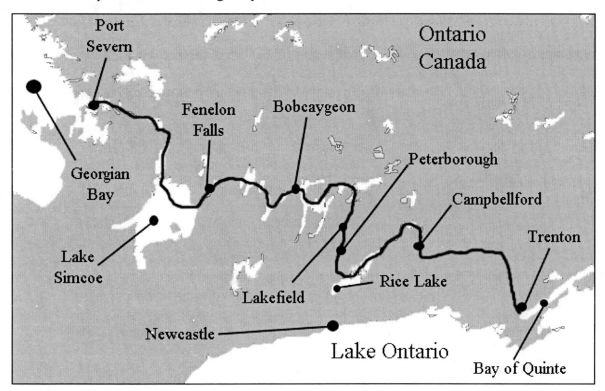

The Trent-Severn Waterway runs from Trenton on Lake Ontario to Port Severn on the Georgian Bay.

The Trent-Severn Waterway is made up of 44 locks, numbered 1 to 45. Lock 29 does not exist as it was combined with 28 into a double hydraulic lock. Lock 44, Big Chute, is not really a lock, but a marine railway. So in all probability you will traverse 42 locks on a trip through the 240 miles of the Trent-Severn Waterway.

The controlled clearance through the Trent-Severn is 22'. Bridges with a height greater than 22' are not listed since you cannot transit the canal if you cannot clear 22'. The controlling depth over the sill is 6'; if your draft is more than 5' you must contact the Trent-Severn Waterway Office office in Peterborough at 705-750-4900 and obtain approval to enter. Captains with

Cruising The Trent Severn Waterway, Georgian Bay, and North Channel
Chapter 3 - The Trent Severn Canal

vessels drawing more than 4 ½ feet should be prepared to sign damage waivers, releasing the Waterway from responsibility.

The Trent-Severn Waterway is usually open from mid May to mid October. During peak summer days the canal portion (bridges and locks) operates from 8:30AM to 7:00PM. If your plans include travel on the Trent-Severn Waterway early or late in the boating season be sure to check with canal personal to see what the operating hours of the locks and bridges are during that period. (Note: See appendix 2 for 2008 operating hours and fees)

As you approach each lock, you will see a stretch of wall or dock painted blue. This "blue line" is the area where boats waiting to go through the lock tie up. Vessels tying up overnight or for a few hours can use all other walls, not painted blue. If you arrive after the lock has closed for the day, you may tie up overnight on the blue line as long as you are prepared to go through the lock at its first opening.

The only lock that responds to a VHF radio call is Lock 1; hail the lock tender on VHF channel 14. Within the system lock tenders rely on telephone communications between locks and bullhorns to direct traffic. This is another reason why it is imperative to adhere to the blue line regulations.

This is a good time to discuss VHF radio operation. In this area of Canada, Channel 12 is used as the "Seaway" channel. You will hear the St. Lawrence Seaway using it. Channel 14 is for contacting bridges, 16 for hailing and 68 for contacting marinas. Be certain you have your radio set to the Canadian channels.

Always tell the lock personnel your plans. They call ahead via phone and alert the bridges and locks of your approach. If you are planning on stopping and spending the night above a lock, be sure to tell the lockmaster.

For planning purposes, you should bear in mind that weekends are the busiest time on the waterway. At that time you not only have transient cruisers and those on holiday, but also most of the locals out on the water. To make your trip more enjoyable, plan your travel between weekends and holidays. Leave on Monday and travel at your leisure Monday through Friday mid day. By Friday mid day find yourself a pleasant lock or community where you can stay for the weekend. Plan on sitting tight and watch all the fun in the locks. The first time you see someone with a rented houseboat attempt to enter and tie up at a lock you will understand my recommendation not to travel on weekends.

For most of the canal portion of the waterway the posted speed limit is 10 KM/Hr. That equates to 6 MPH. The speed limit signs are clearly posted showing both the beginning and the end of the speed limit area.

Bridges along the Trent-Severn Waterway that must open to allow passage do not generally have radios, nor do they have blue lines where you can tie up. The bridge tenders are usually very observant and generally have been alerted by the previous lock or bridge that you passed through that you are coming. However, if the bridge does not show a sign of opening as you approach, slow to idle speed and sound three short blasts on your horn.

In general all of the locks on the Trent-Severn Waterway are manually operated. In these cases, the lock tender must walk the controls around in a circle turning a gear mechanism to open or close the lock gates and the water valves. We will identify the few locks that are operated hydraulically for you.

Do Not Use For Navigation

Cruising The Trent Severn Waterway, Georgian Bay, and North Channel
Chapter 3 - The Trent Severn Canal

Vessels tie up inside the lock to steel cables, spaced about 12 feet apart, that are secured to the lock wall at both the top and bottom of the lock. The cables are coated with rubber so that your lines will not chafe when sliding up or down the line. Make sure there are at least two large fenders on the side of your vessel that will be against the wall. One fender should be forward and one aft. Locking up is a simple matter of coming alongside a cable amidship. Tie a line to a cleat amidship on your vessel. Pass the bitter end of the line around behind the cable suspended on the lock wall. Loop the bitter end of the line to the same cleat amidship and hold the bitter end. Now as the lock raises your vessel the line slides up the steel cable but holds your vessel firmly against the lock wall. **Do not leave the line unattended**. If it should get caught on something you want to be able to release it immediately. In addition, on some of the locks the side of your vessel will rise a good way above the top of the lock wall where the steel cable is attached. When you approach the top you must let out additional line to allow for this.

The channel in the Trent-Severn Waterway is marked with red and green buoys. The rule "Red Right Returning" applies to the first part of the waterway in either direction. Going north from Trenton the channel markers start red on your starboard or right and green on port or left. They remain this way until you reach Kirkfield Lift Lock at mile 169.3. At that point the markers switch sides as you are "returning to the sea" and red is on your left or port and green is on your right or starboard. Buoys here are small and can be difficult to see in a light haze or rain. Do not rely on shape alone to identify a buoy. It is advisable to have a chart plotter onboard with the appropriate area charts. Finally, many buoys that were deemed "non-essential" have been removed as a cost saving measure. So pay attention when navigating and come to a stop if you uncertain about what lies ahead.

The charts are marked with statute mile marker reference points all along the favored route. The markers go from 0 in Trenton to 240 in Port Severn. We will use the statue mile markers throughout chapters 4 to 8 to reference points of interest, locks, etc.

As you begin the waterway there are two significant financial considerations regarding fees you must make decisions about. One is lockage and the other is dockage.

Canal Fees

All of the canals in Canada charge for the use of the locks. They do not charge for the use of the canals. Thus, all fees are in terms of "locking days". A "locking day" is any day that you go through one or more locks. You can use one "locking day" and traverse 10 locks, or you can use one locking day and traverse 2 locks. If you cruise around on the canal and/or lakes between locks and do not go through a lock, you have not used any "locking days".

There are five different lockage plans for pleasure craft (see appendix 2). The plan most appropriate for "loopers" is the seasonal "Transit One Way" pass, which for 2008 is $4.45/ft. Canadian. If you are cruising in the area and plan a return from Georgian Bay or plan to cruise other canals, the "Seasonal Pass" is best.

All locking passes are good for all Canadian Historic Canals. Thus, you can use the same annual locking pass on the Trent-Severn Waterway, Rideau Canal, Lachine Canal, Richelieu Canal, Chambly Canal, and Sault Ste Marie locks, provided you visit these waterways in the same year or season.

The second financial consideration is dockage. Or as the Canadians call it, "mooring". You basically have three options. Anchor out, tie to a lock wall, or stay in a marina. Anchoring out is

Cruising The Trent Severn Waterway, Georgian Bay, and North Channel
Chapter 3 - The Trent Severn Canal

not a problem in some stretches of the waterway where there are lakes and ample wide water with quiet pristine anchorages. However, with anchoring out you miss the great towns and villages at each lock. Marinas are an option. Most of the marinas on the Trent-Severn are small and cater to local boats so it is wise to call well in advance to secure dockage. In certain areas transient dockage is at a premium. Transient rates generally run from $1.00 to $1.75/foot and most times includes hydro.

Krogen trawler at mooring.

Your best bet is to plan on spending most nights on the Trent-Severn tied to a lock wall or town dock with occasional marina stops. For ease of planning, we will only list those marinas that accept transient vessels in the 36' and above range.

If you elect to tie up at the lock walls every night, you will have no problem finding space and being safe and comfortable. Overnight mooring within the canal system requires a "mooring permit" (see Appendix 2). For a single night it is $0.90/ft. Canadian. The 2008 seasonal pass is $9.80/ft. If you are cruising and plan to return from Georgian Bay in the same year, the seasonal mooring pass is most certainly your best bet. Keep in mind that the seasonal mooring pass is valid on all Canadian Historic canals and at all parks operated by Parks Canada. That includes the park at Beausoleil Island in the Georgian Bay as well as the Canadian National Parks in the Thousand Islands.

One final note on the mooring pass. There are restrictions as to how long you can remain at each lock. This rule is in place to avoid having people come in and set up at one lock for a couple of weeks while on summer vacation. It is important to note that the rules about overnight stays are loosely enforced at times. In general if you are not a nuisance and don't stay for a prolonged period, you can plan on staying where you want for as long as you want. That said, here is the restriction. "No vessel will remain at a lock wall more than 48 hours. After departure that vessel may not return to that lock wall for 24 hours." That has been further modified by a written exception for locks 1 to 18 allowing a stay of 5 nights at those locks. Further restrictions have been added to locks 28,30,31,34 and 42 restricting the overnight stay to only one night there. To make your trip easier in chapters 4 to 8 we have listed how long you may stay at each lock. After the expression "overnight mooring" you will find a number enclosed by two special brackets, i.e. [5]. The "5" in the preceding example means overnight mooring is permitted for 5 consecutive days at that lock. However, as we have experienced staying an extra night or two is generally not a problem unless the waterway is extremely busy or there is a special activity planned at that community.

One other way to save money is to purchase the Pre-Season Package before March 31 each year. This package is available directly from the Trent-Severn Waterway National Historic Site, PO Box 567, Peterborough, Ontario K9J 6Z6, phone 1-888-773-8888, or Fax 1-705-742-9644.

Coverage of the Trent Seven Waterway is divided into five sections in the next five chapters. In each chapter the characteristics of the waterway are described and a mile by mile summary highlights navigational concerns, places to stop and visit and historical information. At each lock we identify which side the blue line(s) is on, if there is mooring space available and how much, what facilities are located within walking distance, and what the lift is in feet. The lift in feet will

Do Not Use For Navigation

Cruising The Trent Severn Waterway, Georgian Bay, and North Channel
Chapter 3 - The Trent Severn Canal

be indicated behind the lock name in parentheses; i.e. (8') means an 8-foot lift or drop. The location of each bridge that is less than 22' is also given with the closed height above normal water level in parentheses; i.e. (12') means there is normally 12 feet of clearance with the bridge closed.

The following charts are required to navigate the Trent-Severn Canal (See appendix 1):

Canadian Hydrographic Charts 2021, 2022, 2023, 2024, 2025, 2028 and 2029.

Cruising The Trent Severn Waterway, Georgian Bay, And North Channel

Chapter 4
Trenton to Rice Lake

The first stretch of the Trent-Severn Waterway follows the Trent River upstream from Trenton on Lake Ontario to Rice Lake. The waterway is marked by channel buoys within the wide river keeping the cruiser in deep water. Remember that the rule "Red Right Returning" applies and red markers will be on your right or starboard. While the waterway is fairly wide in places it is also generally very shallow out of the channel. The bottom is mud and anchoring is good in the few wide spots that are deep enough. The countryside is rural and residential. Much of the way there is a road on one side of the canal and a railroad on the other. The small towns of Campbellford and Hastings break up this 51-mile trip through otherwise rural countryside.

The first section of this waterway is dotted with locks. One nearly every mile. Soon the pace will slow down and the locks come further apart. What follows is a mile-by-mile explanation of what to expect as you proceed upstream. All of it keyed to the statute mile markers found on your charts.

Directions in the following four chapters do not necessarily correspond to true compass directions. Rather, the Trent-Severn Waterway is considered to run north and south. Thus when directions are given referring to the "west" it means that it is on port or the left side of your vessel when north bound. Of course that means something to the "west" will be on starboard or your right side if you are south bound.

Fraser Park Marina (613-394-2561, 613-965-1170,G,D,P) is located on the west shore in Trenton. (See page 11 under Arrival in Canada.)

Chart 2021, Sheet 2 of 4

Mile 0.0. The first bridge, The Gateway to the Trent Bridge, is a 28' high fixed bridge and presents no problem for the boater.

Mile 0.4, Railroad Swing Bridge (10'). This bridge has been removed.

Mile 1.7, Lock 1 Trenton (18'). The only lock that uses VHF 14 to communicate with boaters. Lock 1 is isolated and residential with no services nearby. The train noise from the nearby bridge will disturb some boaters. On the lower side there is ample room to tie up 8 boats on either the east or west wall just before the spot where the waterway narrows at the lock. The blue line is on the east wall (starboard) just after the waterway narrows and before the railroad bridge. On

Lock 1 mooring wall upper side.

the upper side (preferred tie up) of the lock there is room for 5 boats to tie up for overnight mooring [5] on the west wall just past the blue line. There is also a pier sticking out into the river on the east side with room for two boats on either side. The lock offers

Cruising The Trent-Severn Waterway, Georgian Bay, And North Channel
Chapter 4 – Trenton to Rice Lake

picnic tables and restrooms. The first gate is operated hydraulically while the second (upper) gates are manual.

Mile 2.4, Lock 2 Sydney (19'). Follow the channel to the east side of the river for the lock entrance. This lock is rural and isolated with a mile long access road. The road noise from the 401 bridge goes on around the clock. On the lower side the blue line is on the east wall. There is mooring space for two boats overnight [5] in front of the blue line on the east wall and three boats on the pier on the west wall. On the upper side mooring can be found only on the east wall and there is room for at least 2 boats in front and two boats behind the blue line on the east wall. There is a pretty park with picnic tables and rest rooms.

The narrow channels and occasional large vessels can make navigating through the Trent-Severn a real adventure.

Mile 3.7, Lock 3 Glen Miller (28'). **Caution**, the entrance to the lock is on the east or starboard side of the bridge just below the lock and is marked by yellow lights. Quiet at last. Isolated residential area. Lower gate operated hydraulically. Limited overnight mooring [5] available on the lower side, but most boaters favor the upper side. On the lower side the blue line is on the east or starboard wall with room for one boat behind the line. On the upper side the favored mooring is on the east or starboard side with room for 4-5 boats and a park with picnic benches. On the west or port side the blue line is closest to the lock with room for 1-2 boats to moor overnight beyond the blue line. Across the bridge (½ mile) on the west side is a restaurant and small convenience store. Follow the path from the store to one of the largest boulders in Ontario deposited by a glacier.

Mile 4.5 to 4.7. **Caution**, there is a rocky outcrop on the east bank in this stretch, do not hug the red or east side.

Mile 5.2, Lock 4 Batawa (18'). Lock entrance is on starboard or the east bank. Strong currents from dam on lower side. Rural and quiet. Original 85-year-old lock house is used for rest rooms and office. Overnight mooring [5] both above and below the lock is only on the east wall. The blue line is in the center on both walls with room overnight for one boat below the lock and 4 boats above the lock.

Mile 5.5. **Caution,** shoal on west bank, favor the middle of the river from lock 4 to T25.

Mile 6.4, Lock 5 Trent (17'). Rural and isolated. Lock and entrance is on the east bank. Overnight mooring [5] above and below lock. Favored mooring above lock. Below lock blue line is on east wall and room for one boat overnight. On the west wall room for 2-3

Cruising The Trent-Severn Waterway, Georgian Bay, And North Channel
Chapter 4 – Trenton to Rice Lake

boats. Above the lock room for 4 boats on east wall with picnic tables in a park. Blue line above the lock on west wall with room for only 1 boat overnight ahead of the line. The stone building here is an original lockmaster's house.

Mile 7.3, Lock 6 Frankford (17'). Rural and isolated. There is overnight mooring [5] above and below the lock. Favored mooring is on the upper side. On the lower side the blue line is on the east wall with room for 1 or 2 boats ahead of the line for overnight. On the west wall there is room for 4 or 5 boats in a park. Above the lock there is room for 6 boats on the east wall overnight and the blue line is on the west wall with room overnight for 2 boats ahead of the line.

There is a small restaurant and grocery ½ mile north on the east bank. The community of Frankford is more than a mile walk on the west side of the river over the road bridge. There you will find a post office, a grocery, a laundry, a pharmacy, Bank/ATM, LCBO, Beer Store, library, video rental and several restaurants. If you are into pizza, ask the lock tender for the telephone number for delivery to the lock.

Mile 13.3. **Caution,** the area of the waterway named Danger Narrows is appropriately named. There is a lot of rock and debris just outside the channel at this point. Watch you charts and stay in the channel, which, fortunately is well marked.

Chart 2021, Sheet 3 of 4

Mile 13.7, Lock 7 Glen Ross (11') and swing bridge (3'). Located in quiet residential area with a small convenience store across the street. Swing bridge operates in conjunction with the lock. Overnight mooring [5] below the lock on both walls. The blue line is on the east wall with only limited mooring in addition to the blue line. The west wall has room for 4 to 5 boats in a park with picnic benches. Above the lock beyond the swing bridge there is overnight mooring for 6 boats on the west wall near the convenience store. On the east wall is the blue line with room for an additional 2 boats overnight.

Mile 13.9, swing bridge (6'). Opened and abandoned.

Mile 21.7, Blue Hole. Just to west side of the waterway (port headed upstream) behind an island is a protected anchorage. Follow the charted channel around behind the unnamed island at T139. Anchor in 10-15' in a protected scenic spot. This area is larger than it looks on the chart.

Mile 25.0, Jett Island. Southwest of the channel between T177 and T179 near Jett Island is a favored anchorage in 7-8'. Proceed slowly and feel your way in to avoid the charted rock and 4' shoal.

Mile 25.3, Lock 8 Percy Reach (19'). Very isolated and rural. Nearly 15 miles from anywhere. Quiet with overnight mooring [5] for 5 boats both above and below the lock on the west wall. Picnic tables in parks both above and below lock. The blue line is on the east wall both above and below the lock with room for only 1 boat in front of both blue lines. Rest rooms and vending machines.

Cruising The Trent-Severn Waterway, Georgian Bay and North Channel
Chapter 4 – Trenton to Rice Lake

Mile 26.4, Lock 9 Meyers (15'). Rural, isolated and quiet. Room for overnight mooring [5] of 5 boats both above and below the lock on the west walls. Park with picnic tables. Blue lines are on the east walls above and below the lock with room for 1 boat ahead of the blue line in each case. The original lock house was built in 1914.

Caution: Above (north bound) lock 9 a number of cribs exist in the water just out of the channel. Loggers placed these cribs in the waterway as long as 100 years ago. Today their presence is marked by red and green day marks signifying the edge of the channel. Be very careful about going out of the channel near a day mark unless the chart indicates sufficient depth. In many cases these old cribs lie just beneath or just at the waterline and are shown only as a shoal or shallow spot on the chart.

Mile 28.0, Lock 10 Hague's Reach (24'). Rural, isolated and quiet. Room for overnight mooring [5] of 5 boats both above and below the lock on the west walls. Park with picnic tables Blue lines are on the east walls above and below the lock with room for 1 boat ahead of the blue line in each case. Room for 4 boats on north dam face wall above the lock on the west wall. The top of the lock is the favored mooring spot, as there is not as much turbulence as the lower side.

A lock can get very busy!

Chart 2021, Sheet 4 of 4

Mile 29.6, Locks 11 & 12 Ranney Falls (48') and swing bridge (5'). The first set of flight locks. In flight locks when the boat comes out of one lock it is actually entering the next lock. These are typically constructed where a large lift must be achieved in a short distance. **Note** – There is a cement ledge along the side of this lock. Watch your fenders/gunnels while locking.

There is overnight mooring [5] both above and below the set of locks. Below lock 11 on the east wall there is room for 3-4 boats at a park with picnic benches. On the west wall there is room before the blue line for 2-3 boats. Above the double locks there is room for 2 boats on the west wall only in front of the blue line. The swing bridge is operated in conjunction with the locks. The locks are operated hydraulically. There are no services in the area. Most vessels do not stop here, but rather push on to Campbellford. Those that do stay usually stay above the lock since the mooring below the lock is so far from the restrooms.

Cruising The Trent-Severn Waterway, Georgian Bay and North Channel
Chapter 4 – Trenton to Rice Lake

Mile 31.0, Campbellford. The west wall at Old Mill Park allows complimentary dockage during the day, and overnight dockage for a fee, but it is not covered by the Parks Canada mooring permit. Services included with the fee are 15A and 30A electric, water, and showers.

Close by on the west bank include downtown shops, pharmacy, ATM machine, pay phone, pubs and Capers Casual Dining restaurant. Bill's No Frills supermarket is on Canrobert Street, two blocks west on Bridge Street. One mile south on Grand Road is a large Canadian Tire big box retail store.

On east bank at New Municipal Park there is dockage with water and 50A service. You pay for dockage $1.50/ft in 2007 incl. electric) on either side at the Tourist Information building on the west side. Both sides get WiFi, but the further south you are, the better the signal. MacMillian's at New Municipal Park sells fuel, both gas and diesel.

Toonie in Campbellford

Within two blocks are a thrift store, sub shop, restaurants, and a movie theater. Three blocks north on Front Street North is a large IGA supermarket. One mile east on Bridge Street East is The Beer Store and four blocks south on Front Street South is the LCBO.

North of the bridge on the west bank is Turner's Service Station (G,D) that offers overnight docking with water and 30A electric. In 2007 the shore power was not operational. The fuel prices at these two facilities have usually been the same and the least expensive on the waterway.

Of interest to boaters is Harold Carlaw's Military Museum, World's Finest Chocolate Factory Outlet Store, Empire Cheese, Church Key Beer, Westben Art Festival Theater, the antique car and motorcycle show and the $2 Coin Statue in Old Mill Park. Plan to stay a few days in Campbellford, it seems most cruisers do. For additional information visit www.visitcampbellford.ca.

Mile 32.2, Lock 13 Campbellford (23'). Vessels are asked to tie to Port when locking up. Isolated residential with no services. Overnight mooring [5] both above and below the lock in parks with picnic benches. Below the lock mooring for 3 boats on the east wall with the blue line on the west wall. Above the lock mooring for 4 boats on west wall with the blue line on the east wall.

Mile 33.7, Lock 14 Crowe Bay (26'). Vessels are asked to tie to starboard when locking up. Residential and isolated, no services. The lower gate is hydraulic. Overnight mooring [5] is available above and below lock. Mooring below the lock is on west wall with the blue

Cruising The Trent-Severn Waterway, Georgian Bay and North Channel
Chapter 4 – Trenton to Rice Lake

line on east wall. Mooring above the lock is on the east wall with the blue line on west wall. Crowe Bay, actually a small lake, is past this lock with a channel well marked with spar buoys. If the lock walls are full there is a good anchorage off-channel approximately three quarters of a mile north in Crowe Bay beyond marker "T272".

Chart 2022, Sheet 1 of 3.

Mile 36.2, Lock 15 Healey Falls (22') and swing bridge (4'). Vessels are asked to tie on the port side when locking up. Isolated residential area. Below the lock the blue line is on the west side and there is room for one boat ahead of it. There is a long wall on the east side, but the lockmaster reports it to be very turbulent when the lock opens.
  Above the lock there is overnight mooring [5] for 4 boats on the east wall and the blue line is on the west wall with room for 2 boats ahead of it. Mooring is also available in the basin along south wall. The swing bridge is normally open as it is used only by maintenance personnel to access the power plant.

Mile 36.5, Lock 16 and 17 Healey Falls (54'). Hydraulically operated flight locks, isolated and rural. **Note** – There is a cement ledge along the side of this lock. Watch your fenders/gunnels while locking.
  The overnight mooring [5] below the lock can be noisy because you are next to a power plant. There is room for 2 boats on the east wall next to the power plant and also room for 2 on the west wall in front of the blue line. Above the power plant is the more favorable mooring. On the west bank only there is room for about 8 boats in front of the blue line. There is a large park there with picnic tables.

The water falls at Healey Falls

Mile 40.8, Hardy Island. There is a protected anchorage north of T304 behind Hardy Island. When leaving this anchorage it is best to return to the main channel where you entered.

Mile 43.4, Trent River. A public dock is provided on the south shore between T331 and the highway 30 bridge. This 100' long dock has 8' alongside. There are no services there. The community of Trent River on the north shore does have a small grocery store and post office. It is quite a walk via the highway 30 bridge.

Cruising The Trent-Severn Waterway, Georgian Bay and North Channel
Chapter 4 – Trenton to Rice Lake

Mile 45.0, Steam Mill Island. South of Steam Mill Island there is a protected anchorage out of the channel.

Mile 51.2, Lock 18 Hastings (9') and swing bridge (5'). Located in the middle of the village of Hastings, this is a very popular stop. Overnight mooring [5] below the lock is limited to two boats in front of the blue line on the north wall. Mooring above the lock is available for about 9 boats on the north wall with the south wall reserved for the blue line. The swing bridge operates in conjunction with the lock. All facilities are located in the town of Hastings adjacent to the lock on the north side. Within two blocks you have The Beer Store, LCBO, a supermarket, hardware, bank, restaurants, post office, laundry and other shops. Saturday mornings features a farmers market.

Mile 51.3, Hastings. Hastings Village Marina (705-696-3226,P) http://www.hastingsvillage.ca/ on the south bank has transient slips with electric and water pumpout at each slip, washroom, shower and Internet service. Transient rates for 2008 are $1.35/ft with 30A and $1.55/ft with 50A.

Cruising The Trent-Severn Waterway, Georgian Bay, And North Channel

Chapter 5
Ontonabee River and Rice Lake

From Hastings the Trent-Severn Waterway first crosses Rice Lake, and then proceeds up the Ontonabee River to Lakefield. This provides three distinctly different cruising areas. Rice Lake is fairly large, at 20 miles long and 2 ½ miles wide. However it is relatively shallow at about 12'. The bottom is mainly mud. The lower part of the Ontonabee River winds its way slowly from Peterborough to Rice Lake. It is a typical river with muddy banks and many areas of marsh. However, the third area is that short piece of the Ontonabee River that goes from Peterborough to Lakefield. Here the Ontonabee rises rapidly through 8 locks in only 10 miles. The landscape becomes rocky and the bottom less forgiving.

Chart 2022, Sheet 1 of 3.

Example of new-faced lock and walls.

Mile 51.5, Hastings. The entrance to Rice Lake starts immediately west of Hastings. Even though this is marsh country do not be complacent. There are many rocks just below the surface. Stay in the channel.

Mile 56.6, Twin Cedars Cottages (marina) (705-696-3127,G). South shore of Rice Lake in Morrow Bay this resort offers dockage for a couple of 36' boats in 6' of water. Small convenience store.

Chart 2022, Sheet 2 of 3.

Mile 57.0, Rice Lake. The lake really starts here and it opens into a wide body of shallow water where you can boat and play to your hearts content. Be aware that there are a number of shallow areas around the lake, mostly at the eastern end. It is best to do your off the waterway exploring on the western end of Rice Lake. Rice Lake is surrounded by Indian history including the Serpent Mounds Provincial Park and the Hiawatha Reserve. Unfortunately the lake is so shallow and there are no good docks where you can go ashore here to visit these locations.

Mile 58.7, Lang's Resort (marina) (905-352-2308,G,P). On the south shore nearly east of T421 located at McCracken Landing with limited groceries. Room for 4 boats in 5'. Electrical service is 15A.

Mile 66.0, Golden Beach Resort (marina) (905-342-5366,G). On the south shore SE of TRC RW. Look for orange roofs and marina sign. Room for about 40 transient vessels up to 45' long. Shallow harbor at 4' but well protected. Call for instructions before entering harbor. Laundry, propane, 20A elect, and swimming pool.

Cruising The Trent-Severn Waterway, Georgian Bay, And North Channel
Chapter 5 – Ontonabee River and Rice Lake

Caution: If approaching or leaving either Cedar Cove Resort or the public dock at Harwood listed below, be sure to swing wide to the east of Tick Island to avoid the charted shoal.

Mile 66.4, Cedar Cove Resort (marina) (905-342-3110). On the south shore about midway between Sager Point and the end of the old bridge. Room for several transient boats up to 45' long with 6' alongside. 30A elect, showers, swimming pool, and limited groceries in Harwood.

Mile 66.6, Public Dock at Harwood. The government dock at the SSE end of the old bridge has 6' alongside and no other facilities. Limited groceries in the small town of Harwood.

Mile 66.8, Harwood Bridge. **Caution,** the base, or cribs, of the old railroad bridge that used to cross Rice Lake are still located in the water across Rice Lake. The old bridge crossed what is now the Trent-Severn Waterway channel at marker T429. While you may feel free to explore Rice Lake pretty much as you want, watch your charts closely and only cross the old Harwood Bridge cribs in the channel.

Mile 68.6, Otonabee River mouth. At the flashing red marker you turn north between T433 and T434 and head north up the Otonabee River. If you choose to explore more of Rice Lake there are several marinas where you can tie up.

> Audley's Cove Marina (905-342-2138,G,P). On the south shore near Gores Landing. 30A electric and showers. Room for transients 42' long with 6' at the dock. East most marina near charted "piles".

> Gore's Landing Marina (905-342-5783,G,P). On the south shore near Gores Landing. 30A electric, showers and swimming pool. Room for transients 45' long with depth of at least 6'.

> Plank Road Cottages (marina) (905-342-5555,G). On the south shore near Gores Landing between Gores Landing Marina and the charted Public dock. Room for 4 transients of 36' with 6' depth. 15A electric, showers and E-mail hookup.

> Gores Landing provides a small general store with limited groceries.

Chart 2022, Sheet 3 of 3.

Mile 73.8, Campbelltown. Campbelltown provides a 60' public dock 4' high where you can tie up to visit this small community. Wakes during the day, but quiet at night.

Mile 86.3, Rocks Awash. **Caution,** for the next two miles north past marker C49 there are rocks awash just outside the channel. Follow the channel closely in this area.

Mile 88.8, Lock 19 Scott Mills (8'). The major overnight mooring [2] area on the lower side of the lock is on the west side in front of the short blue line. Room for about 4 boats. The

Cruising The Trent-Severn Waterway, Georgian Bay, And North Channel
Chapter 5 – Ontonabee River and Rice Lake

entire east wall is a blue line. The preferred mooring is found above the lock on the west wall just past the blue line but before the fixed bridge. There is room for about 4 boats. Located in a residential area only a few blocks from many Peterborough restaurants and stores.

Mile 88.9, Railroad Bridge (9'). Normally open unless train is coming.

Mile 89.4, Peterborough Marina (705-745-8787, G, D, P). Transient up to 80', 9' depth reported, 50A electric, showers. Located on the west end of Little Lake in downtown Peterborough. This is an excellent base for visiting Peterborough. A couple of blocks from the downtown marina is an enclosed shopping area called Peterborough Square. One block away on George Street is Boater's World, a discount marine parts store. A supermarket, LCBO, Beer Store, banks (ATM), pharmacy and many restaurants are within a 10 min walk. Del Crary Park, adjacent to the marina, is the setting for Summer Festival of Lights, concert and fireworks event beginning at 8 pm every Wednesday and Friday.

You can anchor in Little Lake between the canal channel and the marina. Favor the south side of the lake out of the direct path to the marina and be certain you are clear of the fountain spray in the event of a wind shift.

Mile 89.5, Lock 20 Ashburnham (12'). Residential tree lined park with no services. It is a fifteen-minute walk to downtown Peterborough from here. Overnight mooring [2] for 4 boats below the lock on the east side. The blue line is on the west side both above and below the lock with room for one boat ahead of the blue line below the lock. No overnight mooring above the lock. Below the lock on the west side there is a nice swimming beach located on the shores of Little Lake.

Mile 89.7, Maria Street Swing Bridge (4'). Opens in conjunction with the lock.

Mile 89.8, Railroad swing bridge (4'). Normally open unless train is coming.

Mile 90.1, Lock 21 Peterborough Lift Lock (65'). Signal lights tell you which pan to enter. In this lock you get to secure your vessel to the side and not work the lines as you are raised.

Because this is such a busy lock, the painted blue lines are on both walls above and below the lock. No overnight mooring is allowed below the lock. Tie ups on the west wall are for day use only and allow access to the visitor center with its displays and exhibits of the locks history. Above the lock overnight mooring [2] is permitted. You are about one mile

Peterborough Lift Lock.

Cruising The Trent-Severn Waterway, Georgian Bay, And North Channel
Chapter 5 – Ontonabee River and Rice Lake

from downtown Peterborough, and only a short walk to a science museum.

Historical Note. The Peterborough Lift Lock was completed in 1904 and was considered an engineering marvel at that time. Each of the two pans weighs 1300 tons when filled. With one pan up and the other down the two balance each other. It does not matter how many boats are in either pan. A boat displaces its own weight in water. When it is time to lower one pan and raise the other, one extra foot of water (130 tons) is allowed to enter the upper pan. This extra weight allows the upper pan to push down and raise the lower pan to the top level. The two pans are locked in place and the extra water is let out of the lower pan. Boats enter and exit the upper and lower pans and the process is repeated.

Chart 2023, Sheet 1 of 3.

Mile 91.0, Guard Gate and Warsaw Road Swing Bridge (5'). The bridge opens on request and the Guard Gate is open unless the Peterborough Lift Lock is closed for service.

Mile 93.4, Railroad Swing Bridge (8'). Always open, train line abandoned.

Mile 94.2, Lock 22 Nassau Mills (14'). Rural pristine setting. Preferred overnight mooring [2] for 2 boats is above the lock on the east bank next to a park with picnic tables. There is also overnight mooring for 10 boats on the west bank above the lock next to the blue line, but no park or tables, and the area is not well maintained. Below the lock the blue line is on the west wall with no overnight mooring available during the normal hours of lock operation.

Mile 94.7, Lock 23 Otonabee (12'). Rural almost pristine setting. Below the lock there is overnight mooring [2] for 2-3 boats on the west wall, but there are only a few rings and bollards to tie to. Generally not a good overnight stop. On the east wall one boat in front and one boat behind the blue line. Above the lock overnight mooring for 4 boats on the east side beyond the blue line with access to picnic tables and grills.

Mile 96.4, Lock 24 Douro (12'). Residential setting, no services. Overnight mooring [2] for 3 boats both above and below the lock on the west wall. Above the lock is the preferred mooring. Blue line is on the east wall both above and below the lock.

Mile 97.3, Lock 25 Sawyer Creek (10'). Rural setting. Below the lock is not recommended for overnight mooring [2] although there is room for 3 boats on the west wall. The east wall is just the blue line. Overnight mooring above the lock is available on the west wall with picnic tables. There is also room for two boats in front of the blue line on the east wall. There is significant dam noise above the lock.

Chart 2023, Sheet 2 of 3.

Mile 98.7, Lock 26 Lakefield (16'). Residential area. Lakefield is about a one-mile walk from the lock (see description below at mile 99.1.). Below the lock the blue line occupies the north side and there is no room for overnight mooring [2]. There is room for 3 or 4 boats on the

Cruising The Trent-Severn Waterway, Georgian Bay, And North Channel
Chapter 5 – Ontonabee River and Rice Lake

south side below the lock, but it is rarely used, as the area above the lock is preferred. Lots of overnight mooring above the lock on the north side. Room for 6 or more boats beyond the blue line. Room for 3 or 4 boats on the south side as well.

Mile 98.7 to 99.0. **Caution,** very narrow gorge with little room to pass another vessel.

Mile 99.1, Lakefield. There are walls on both sides just past the bridge with overnight mooring [2] for 9 or 10 boats. The north side is closer to the park, trees and tables, while the south side is closer to town. Neither wall is part of Parks Canada and overnight mooring is $1.25/ft (2006). Mooring during the day is free. It is a short walk across the river to Lakefield on the north side. Immediately across the bridge there is a large IGA supermarket, ice cream store, hardware store, shops, bank, library and restaurant. There is a Beer Store on Queen Street about one mile north. There is also a LCBO at Nicholas and Water Streets. **Historical note.** Visit the old Christ Church on Queen Street, right downtown. First put in service in 1854, it is over 150 years old.

One of the widest vessels ever taken through the Trent-Severn Canal. This new ferry was made so that it was just inches narrower than the locks on the Trent-Severn Canal. In fact one side of the new ferry is actually up on the deck of the ferry in this photo. Once this ferry is put in service on one of the lakes of the Trent-Severn Canal, that side will be moved down and welded in place. Then the ferry will be wider than the locks on the Trent-Severn Canal and the ferry will forever be trapped on that lake.

Chapter 6
Kawartha Lakes

Above Lakefield to Balsam Lake you enter the area referred to as Kawartha Lakes. This area has long been a vacation spot for Canadians and abounds in lakeside homes, cottages, boating and recreational activities. It is characterized by a series of lakes joined by locks. The terrain is often rocky, the homes and cottages beautiful.

This area also abounds in history. The first lock on the Trent-Severn Waterway was built at Bobcaygeon in 1833. Native Indians traveled these waterways by canoe more than 3 thousand years ago.

In between the lakes are sprinkled the great little tourist towns of Burleigh Falls, Buckhorn, Bobcaygeon, and Fenelon Falls. Most cruisers find the Kawartha Lakes to be the highlight of their trip through the Trent-Severn.

Chart 2023, Sheet 2 of 3.

Mile 100.6, Lakefield Marina (705-652-0330,P). On the east shore just before the waterway breaks out into Katchewanooka Lake. Newly renovated, 16 transient slips are equipped with 30A/50A electric. Downtown Lakefield is a 5 block walk.

Mile 104.9, Lock 27 Young's Point (7'). Operated hydraulically. Below the lock there is overnight mooring [2] for 5 boats on the west wall before the blue line and 1 more boat on the east wall before a

A quiet overnight mooring on a lock in the Trent-Severn Canal

second blue line. There is mooring for 5 boats above the lock on the west wall beyond the blue line. There is also room for 3 boats on the east wall.

Note – Tie your boat to shore by looping a line through the cleat and back to the boat as reports have been received of children untying boats here. There are picnic tables and a park as well as a walking bridge to the other side of this cottage community. Located in a tourist community filled with cottages and several small stores. Right at the lock is the Lockside Trading Co. which provides gifts and unique shopping as well as ice cream. Located adjacent to the Trading Co, is the Old Bridge Inn that provides pies, french fries, pizza, ice cream, etc. One block north there is the Snack Shack, post office, and general grocery store.

Mile 104.6, Youngs Point Marina (705-652-8563,G). On the west shore opposite C182. Room for two transient vessels in 6' of water. 15A electric, and restrooms.

Cruising The Trent-Severn Waterway, Georgian Bay, And North Channel
Chapter 6 – Kawartha Lakes

Mile 108.0, Clear Lake. **Caution,** Clear Lake and Stony Lake abound in rocks both above and below the surface. Follow your charts carefully. Off to the west near mile 108 and "C167" is a rock named The Spoiler. You will not have any problem if you stay in the channel and proceed slowly when out of the channel.

Mile 108.3, Kawartha Park Marina (705-654-3549,G,). Transient vessels to 60'. Reported water depth is 12' and electric is 30A. Located on the west shore.

Mile 109.5 to 110.5, Hells Gate. A lot scarier sounding than it actually is. Follow the charts and you will have no problems. Not near as bad as Hells Gate on Long Island between the Long Island Sound and the East River. In NY the bottom is also all rock, but the current flows in NY at up to 5 knots with the tide. That is scary. There is little current in the Hell Gate in Canada and the scenery through Hells Gate is breathtaking. The channel however, is narrow, so take your time.

Mile 110.6, Stony Lake. If you have time and want to spend time at anchor in absolutely beautiful pristine conditions take the channel at C200 to Stony Lake. Stony Lake provides the same background of rocky hillsides and islands that you will see in the Georgian Bay. Use Chart 2023, sheet 3 of 3. Fishing is great, the scenery to die for and the quiet mind numbing. There are many quiet anchorages with just your name on it in Stony Lake. A number of public docks are marked on shore and on islands around Stony Lake. Loading/unloading and short stays are OK, but do not plan to stay overnight or a prolonged period.

McCrackens Landing on the west shore has a small but well equipped general store (Choate Supply Store) with groceries and limited marine supplies. To the south a short distance is Carveth's Marina (705-652-6226,G,) with limited transient space, but does have propane.

If you are looking for a large resort marina, Stony Lake offers one at Mount Julian. Follow the red dotted channel markers (chart 2023, sheet 3 of 3) to the north shore of Stony Lake, north of McCrackens Landing. A bit off the waterway but well worth the stop if a stay at an upscale marina and resort (Viamede Resort (705-652-1166,P) is in your budget. Room for more than 30 large transient vessels in 6' of water. Restaurant, 30A electric, swimming pool, and E-mail hookup.

Mile 112.9, Lock 28 Burleigh Falls (24'). Isolated but with busy highway. Vending machines but no other services. Below the lock (actually north) there is overnight mooring [1] for 4 boats on the west side. The blue line on the east wall. Above the lock there is mooring on the west side for 3 boats. On the east wall after the blue line there is room for 3 boats. This lock operates hydraulically.

Historical note. There is no Lock 29. Burleigh Falls used to have two locks. The newer lock replaced both 28 and 29.

Mile 114.7, Lock 30 Lovesick (6'). This lock is really unique in that it is only accessible by boat. It is totally isolated with no services. Operated hydraulically. Below the lock (north side)

Do Not use For Navigation

Cruising The Trent-Severn Waterway, Georgian Bay, And North Channel
Chapter 6 – Kawartha Lakes

there is overnight mooring [1] for 4 boats before the blue line on the east wall. There is mooring for 4 boats above the lock on the east side next to the park. The blue line is on the west side. There is usually a resident flock of Canada Geese here that makes the wall walkway rather messy to walk on.

Mile 118.7, Reach Harbour. On the shore near marker C273 is Reach Harbour Marina (705-657-8747,G,P,WiFi). Room for several transient vessels, but only 4-5' alongside. 50A electric.

Chart 2024, Sheet 1 of 5.

Mile 120.7, Lock 31 Buckhorn (11'). Lock is hydraulic. Below the lock (north) there is overnight mooring [1] for 3 boats only on the east side with the blue line on the west side. Mooring for 10 boats above the lock both east and west just past the blue lines which are also on both the east and west walls.

> Residential area. Across the bridge about ½ mile from the lock on the east side is a large hardware store, grocery and bakery. On the west side there are two restaurants a block away. A small general store, pharmacy, LCBO, library and pizzeria are ¾ mile away on the west side.

Mile 121.5, Buckhorn Yacht Harbour (705-657-8752,G,D,P). On the north shore at Hall Point. Room for a number of larger transient vessels with 6' at the fuel dock and 4 ½' in the slips. 30A electric and showers.

Mile 126.5, Fox Island. Note that the main Trent-Severn Waterway passes to the west of Fox Island. There is an interesting side trip south through Harrington Narrows. However the channel is generally very weedy and probably not what most cruisers are interested in. On this alternate route, almost due east of Fox Island is Coppaway Point. One quarter of a mile northeast from that point along the shoreline is the Whetung Ojibwa Crafts and Art Gallery dock. The water at the dock is 6' but can be weedy. However you can anchor off and dinghy to the dock to see the interesting selection of Indian art and crafts.

> If you should take the side trip southeast through Harrington Narrows, you will need chart 2024, sheet 3. This path takes you to Chemong Lake and Upper Chemong Lake. Chemong Lake provides a deep clear channel to the community of Bridgenorth, just south of the 22' fixed bridge shown on your chart. Just 2 blocks away from the bridge on Ward Street is the plaza with a hardware store, pharmacy, supermarket, bank (ATM), post office and assorted other shops. There is also the Beer Store/LCBO on Ward Street.

> Dutch Marine (705-292-7111,G,D,P) east of the bridge on the south shore provides space for transients up to 36' with depths of 6'. 30A electric, and showers.

> Mars Marina (705-292-6840,G,P) east of the bridge on the north shore provides space for transients up to 42' with depths of 6'. 15A electric, and showers.

Cruising The Trent-Severn Waterway, Georgian Bay, And North Channel
Chapter 6 – Kawartha Lakes

Chart 2024, sheet 4 of 5.

Mile 131.5, Pigeon Lake. Most of this chart is made up of the south end of Pigeon Lake and this end of Pigeon Lake is too shallow and weedy to be of much interest to cruisers.

Chart 2024, sheet 2 of 5.

Mile 132.0, Pigeon Lake. The stretch between Gannon Narrows and Bobcaygeon is deep and easy to traverse. The wooded hills remind you more of Michigan than the Georgian Bay.

Chart 2024, sheet 5 of 5.

Mile 137.0, Pigeon Lake. This chart really only is necessary if you want to explore some of the northeast portion of Pigeon Lake. Your main objective here is to make the turn to the west into Bobcaygeon and the next chart.

Chart 2025, sheet 1 of 3.

Mile 137.9, Gordon Yacht Harbour (705-738-2381,G,P, WiFi). On the north shore before C356 is the Gordon Yacht Harbour Marina. 30A electric, showers and E-mail hookup.

Mile 138.2, Lock 32 Bobcaygeon (6') and swing bridge (11'). The lock is operated hydraulically. Very busy and narrow channel. There is overnight mooring [2] for 8 boats below the lock and before the swing bridge on the south wall. The blue line is at the head of this south wall. There is also room for 4 boats on the north wall. Above the lock there is room for 5 boats beyond the blue line on the south wall. There is overnight mooring for 5 boats on north wall. Above the lock there are picnic benches and a park on both sides of the waterway.
    The Beer Store and LCBO, are ½ mile north of lock on King Street. Within two blocks on the south side of the lock you have banks, laundromat, restaurants, pharmacy and an IGA supermarket.
    Note – A couple of boats reported being untied at night at this stop. Be sure to tie from the boat thru a cleat and back to the boat.

Mile 139.2, Centre Point Landing Marina (705-738-3463,G,P). On north shore north of C374 this marina has transient dockage for 8 vessels with 5' of water, laundromat and shower.

Mile 140.5, Birch Point Marina (705-738-2473,G,P). Midway between C384 and C382 on the south shore this marina provides transient dockage for larger vessels in 5' of water. 30A electric and showers.

Mile 148.2, Sturgeon Lake. There is a side trip available to the community of Lindsay south on the Scugog River. Chart 2026 is required for this side trip. Your vessel must be able to clear **a fixed bridge of 13.5'** to get to lock 33 and another fixed bridge of 11' to go beyond Lindsay to Port Perry on Lake Scugog. It is doubtful if any cruisers will be

Cruising The Trent-Severn Waterway, Georgian Bay, And North Channel
Chapter 6 – Kawartha Lakes

interested in this side trip. Lindsay does provide some very good shopping, but that is seldom a good reason for this type of side trip.

Mile 153.6, Lock 34 Fenelon Falls. Located in the center of the busy tourist town of Fenelon Falls. The lock is operated hydraulically and is one of the newer ones on the system. Below the lock there is overnight mooring [1] on the south wall on both sides of the finger pier. There is room for about 8 boats here with a great view of the falls and the restaurant located on the falls. On the north wall there is only the blue line. Above the lock there is overnight mooring for 4 boats on the south wall beyond the blue line and room for 2 boats on the short north wall.

Fenelon Falls.

On the north side alongside the lock are two restaurants, with a third just around the corner on May Street. The Liquor Store is at the corner of May and Francis West. On the south side of the lock is a restaurant overlooking the falls. Beside it is the Sobey's Supermarket and a Tim Hortons'. Three blocks south of the lock is the Beer Store and another block to the Canadian Tire and Home Center (hardware).

Mile 153.7, swing bridge (6'). Former train bridge is left open during the boating season.

Mile 154.0, Fenelon Falls Marina (705-887-4022,G,P). Along the shoreline on your port as you come out of the cut at Fenelon Falls. 15A electric and showers.

Chart 2025, sheet 2 of 3.

Mile 157.2, Lock 35 Rosedale (4'). Isolated summer cottage setting. Vending machines and restrooms. Hydraulically operated. Below the lock overnight mooring [2] for 13 boats on the south side in picnic park. On north side is the blue line with room for two boats in front. Above the lock room overnight for 5 boats in park on north side. On south side the blue line with room for 2 boats in front.

Mile 157.9, Rosedale Marina (705-887-6921,G,D,P). On the north wall of the canal before the bridge is the Rosedale Marina with room for 10 transient vessels up to 42' and 4 ½' draft. 30A electric, showers and laundry.

Mile 158.1, Rosedale. Public dock on the north shore just past the bridge with 5' alongside. The Community of Rosedale offers a small grocery and deli.

Cruising The Trent-Severn Canal, Georgian Bay, And North Channel

Chapter 7
The Talbot River

Balsam Lake to Lake Simcoe has the boater follow the route of the Talbot River and the many man made canals that connected various lakes to get there. At first the waterway passes through Balsam Lake, the highest point of the Trent-Severn Waterway. Next you enter the cuts which were the last canals made to complete the Trent-Severn in 1920. This is followed by a trip down a canal to Lake Simcoe. he Trent-Severn drops more than 120 feet in just 12 miles. You will be busy locking on that day.

Chart 2025, sheet 2 of 3.

Mile 158.0, Balsam Lake. At this point you are more than 840 feet above sea level and at the highest point in the Trent-Severn Waterway. Whether north or south bound you will lock down for the remainder of your trip on the Trent-Severn Waterway. For those that want to anchor out, there are plenty of places to do it on Balsam Lake where you can seek protection from any wind direction.

Mile 158.4, Coboconk. 5 miles north of where the Trent-Severn enters Balsam Lake is the town of Coboconk. There is a public dock on the port side in town and an grocery within easy walk as well as other shops and restaurants.

Chart 2025, sheet 3 of 3.

Mile 163.4, Trent Canal. On the west side of Balsam Lake the Trent-Severn Waterway enters one of those narrow rock cuts all cruisers dread. This canal is a land cut through the Canadian Shield, a geological feature that covers half the country. It is shallow and narrow. Make a security call prior to entering. Hold your speed to 5 mph. If following another vessel drop back at least 50 yards to allow the drift that is stirred up to settle. If you meet a vessel head on be extremely cautious when passing and come to a complete stop if necessary.

Kirkfield Lift Lock.

Mile 166.0 to 167.2, Mitchell Lake. **Caution,** this lake is full of stumps and very shallow. Stay in the channel.

Mile 167.2 to 168.5, Trent Canal. Now the narrow rock walls even take a turn to the west. Are you having fun yet?

Cruising The Trent-Severn Canal, Georgian Bay, And North Channel
Chapter 7 – The Talbot River

Mile 169.3, Lock 36 Kirkfield Lift Lock (49'). This is more thrilling than the trip up the Peterborough Lock. The lift structure is not enclosed and you get more of a feeling of "hanging out there". To make matters worse, if you are north bound (as most first time users of the Trent-Severn Waterway are), you proceed out into a pan suspended nearly 5 stories in the air. If you are afraid of heights, this lock is sure to thrill you. This lock is remote and isolated in a rural setting. There is a small restaurant across the road from the lock office. The access road goes under the upper part of the canal so in effect you are on an aqueduct for 50 feet.

Boats in the pan at Kirkfield.

Above the lock there is overnight mooring [2] for 10 boats on each side of the lock before the blue lines, which are also on both sides of the lock. Above the lock you are exposed to winds and it may not be pleasant in a heavy blow. Below the lock there is again plenty of room on both sides of the canal for 5 boats protected from the winds. The overnight mooring is after the blue lines, which are also on both sides.

The town of Kirkfield is a two-mile walk west along the highway. A small convenience store, LCBO/Beer Store, pharmacy, post office and restaurants are located there.

Caution, green and red markers change sides at this point. North bound green is now on your right or starboard (you are returning to sea). South bound the same rule applies.

Mile 170.0, Canal Lake. This is another man-made lake with shallows, extreme weed growth in the channel and many submerged dead heads. Go slowly and use the same precautions that you used in the Trent Canal. Wind here can blow you out of the channel without your noticing it. This channel condition continues until mile 173.0.

Hole in the Wall Bridge

Mile 173.0, Hole in the Wall Bridge. Constructed in 1905, vertical clearance is 28 feet. Once past the bridge the channel widens just a bit. Be careful as all of the navigational aids between here and mile 174.8 were removed in 2007. This section of the lake has been overrun with thick, long weeds and if you find yourself slowing down you may have weeds tangled around your props.

Do Not Use For Navigation

Cruising The Trent-Severn Waterway, Georgian Bay, And North Channel
Chapter 7 - The Talbot River

Mile 175.3, swing bridge (5'). Opens on request.

Note: It is about a 2-mile walk to the small community of Bolsover from either of the two marinas below. Bolsover offers a small grocery and pizza.

Mile 176.4, Sunset Cove Marina (705-426-5221,G,P). On the east side. Large transient vessels can be tied up alongside in 5' of water. 30A electric and showers.

Mile 176.6, Port of Call Marina (705-426-7522,G,P). On the SE bank just before the swing bridge is the Port of Call Marina. Room for several transients in more than 8' of water. 30A electric and showers.

Mile 176.7, swing bridge (5'). Opens on request.

Mile 177.1, Lock 37 Bolsover. Isolated residential area. Above the lock there is overnight mooring [2] for 3 boats on the south wall. The north wall is only a blue line, but there is room for 2 boats on the back side of the wall. Below the lock there is overnight mooring for 3 boats on the north wall, but it is not recommended due to the turbulence from the lock out flow. The blue line below the lock is on the south wall.

Mile 178.2, Lock 38 Talbot. Secluded residential area on narrow canal. No services. Overnight mooring [2] for 2 boats available above the lock on the south side. The blue line above the lock is on the north side with room for one boat on the end of the right angle wall before the blue line. Below the lock there is no overnight mooring. The blue line is on the south side.

Mile 179.6, Lock 39 Portage. Totally isolated rural setting on narrow canal. Not even road access for the public. Above the lock overnight mooring [2] for 3 boats on the south wall in a park with the blue line on the north side. Below the lock mooring for 3 boats on the north wall with the blue line on the south wall.

Mile 180.2, Lock 40 Thorah. Totally isolated rural setting on narrow canal. Not even road access for the public. Very quiet at night. Above the lock overnight mooring [2] for 4 boats on the south wall in a park with the blue line on the north side. Below the lock there is room for 3 boats on the north side with the blue line on the south wall.

Mile 180.8, Lock 41 Gamebridge. Isolated rural setting on narrow canal. Above the lock overnight mooring [2] for 4 boats on the south wall. The blue line above the lock occupies the entire north wall. Below the lock there is room for three boats on the north wall just before the bridge. The blue line is on the south wall. Highway 12 crosses canal just below the lock along with an active train bridge, which makes this stay a little noisy at night.

Mile 182.2, Lake Simcoe and Lakeshore Road Swing Bridge (10'). The swing bridge opens on request during the hours the Trent-Severn locks open. Just beyond the swing bridge, the canal entrance from Lake Simcoe provides lots of overnight mooring [5] in an isolated

Do Not Use For Navigation

Cruising The Trent-Severn Waterway, Georgian Bay, And North Channel
Chapter 7 - The Talbot River

residential camping area. Piers have been built out into the lake in such a fashion as to protect the first 500 feet of the canal. The mooring walls on either side of the canal have room for 10 boats on each side. There are no services at this location, but it is a good place to wait for a good day to cross Lake Simcoe.

Chart 2028, sheet 1 of 3.

Mile 182.4 to 197.2, Lake Simcoe. This lake, some 20 miles long and 16 miles wide, is the largest lake on the Trent-Severn Waterway. Its open water can create cruising hazards; thunderstorms can bring 8 foot waves and the breakwater entrance can be messy in westerly winds. Always obtain a weather forecast from the Lake Simcoe buoy prior to entering. There are several marinas; the two most common stops for boats are Lagoon City or McPhee Bay.

Lagoon City Marina (705-484-5063,G,D,P) is located 9 miles north of the Trent Canal entrance. Lagoon City consists of homes built on a canal system similar to what you see in Fort Lauderdale, FL. Lagoon City Marina (on port at the first major bend) can handle large vessels requiring a draft of up to 6'. Cable TV, 30A electric, showers and propane.

McPhee Bay is located further north near the top of the lake where the Trent-Severn Waterway leaves the lake. Two marinas are located there to serve transient vessels. Marina del Rey (705-325-3051,P) is located in the privately marked canal at McRae Point Provincial Park. This marina is located on a deep-water canal able to handle larger vessels. 30A electric and showers.
  Further into McPhee Bay in the NE corner is Starport Landing (705-325-3775,G,D,P). This marina can handle larger vessels in 6' of water. 50A electric, showers and swimming pool.

Beaverton Harbour, 2.7 miles south of mile 182.4 where the Trent-Severn Canal enters the west shore of Lake Simcoe, provides a concrete pier on both sides of the channel to tie up to overnight. A short walk to town from the wall on the west side provides access to restaurants, movie, grocery, banks, and shops. Visit the Beaver River Museum nearly at dockside while there.
  Beaverton Yacht Club (705-426-7309,G,P) is located at the end of the channel and can handle 42' vessels with 5' draft. 30A Electric, and showers.

Lake Simcoe is excellent for sailing. However, most cruisers transiting the Trent-Severn Waterway do not have their masts up and their major concern is to get across Lake Simcoe without getting beat up. For this reason we won't go into details on Jacksons Point, Elmhurst Beach, Maskinonge River Entrance, Holland River, or Barrie. Several of these places have full service marinas with diesel and gasoline.

Historical Note – Lake Simcoe is named for Sir John Simcoe who was the first Lieutenant-Governor of Upper Canada in 1791. He is well known for having abolished slavery in 1793, long before America.

Cruising The Trent-Severn Waterway, Georgian Bay, And North Channel
Chapter 7 - The Talbot River

Mile 197.6, The Narrows. This is the northern most corner of Lake Simcoe where you depart Lake Simcoe on the Trent-Severn Waterway headed towards Port Severn. East of the narrows bridge is a convenience store, donut shop and restaurant. West of the narrows bridge is another convenience store, propane fill, and restaurant. Two marinas just south of the fixed bridge are available for larger transient vessels.

On the east shore is Blue Beacon Marina (705-325-2526,G,P). Does not monitor VHF. 30A electric.

On the west shore is Mariner's Point Marina (705-327-0251,P). 30A electric, and showers.

Mile 197.7, railroad swing bridge (7'). Normally open unless train is coming.

Mile 197.8, Hot Knots Landing Marina (705-326-7898,G,D,P). On the west side just before S310 is the marina best equipped for larger vessels. 30A electric, showers, propane, and E-mail hookup. Newly renovated docks, laundry, and flowers in the restrooms.

Mile 198.8, Orillia. Turn west on the marked channel just past S304 for the protected Port of Orillia Marina (705-326-6314). Lots of transient space with 30A electric and showers. Ask about reported shoaling in parts of the marina. Couchiching Beach Park borders the marina. It is a short walk to main street and a large grocery, LCBO, a pharmacy, banks, restaurants and shops.

Mile 199.0 to 205.0, Lake Couchiching. This lake is about 10 mile long and more shallow than Simcoe. A speed limit is not posted until mile 208.0 so powerboats run fast here, at times creating large wakes. Anchorages are available east of Barnfield Point, in Pumpkin Bay and north of Chiefs Island. The water depth is approximately 9 feet, so proceed slowly.

Mile 201.5, Mariposa Beach. East of S298 is the Ojibway Bay Marina (705-326-5855,G,P). Room for transient vessels (6') and provides 30A electric, showers, and laundry. Adjacent to Casino Rama with gambling casino, restaurant with complimentary meal for transient boaters, convenience store, and pharmacy.

Mile 208.2, McGregor Marina (705-689-9935,G,P). West shore just before Orillia Island. **Caution:** The entrance to this marina is located along the west breakwater at S260. You **do not** want to try to enter this marina south from the open waters of the lake. Room for 5 larger transient vessels in 5' of water. 30A electric, and showers.

Mile 208.3, Orillia Island. The end of Lake Couchiching and the beginning of the final stretch of the Trent-Severn Waterway.

Do Not Use For Navigation

Cruising The Trent-Severn Waterway, Georgian Bay, And North Channel
Chapter 7 - The Talbot River

Entrance to the lock at Fenelon Falls, mile 153.6

Narrow channel on Balsam Lake

Cruising The Trent-Severn Waterway, Georgian Bay, And North Channel

Chapter 8
The Severn River

The final section of the Trent-Severn Waterway is the Severn River. The low lying farm land gives way to breath taking granite rock formations. Heavily forested and isolated, this section of the waterway will prepare you for the North Channel. You can anchor out on clear water in quiet solitude or tie up at a marina or lock. The nights are cool, fishing and swimming is great, cruising is wonderful and all is right with the world.

Chart 2028, sheet 2 of 3.

Mile 208.0. The Trent Canal takes you through a narrow cut to join the Severn River and your downhill run to Port Severn.

Mile 209.2, railroad swing bridge (14'). Normally open unless train is coming.

Mile 209.9, Lock 42 Couchiching (21'). Residential area. Hydraulically operated. Above the lock there is overnight mooring [1] for 3 boats on the west wall. The blue line above the lock is on the east wall and there is room for 2 boats before the blue line. Below the lock there is overnight mooring for 4 boats on the west wall next to a park. The blue line below the lock is on the east wall and there is room for 1 boat overnight beyond the blue line. There is a bridge virtually overhead of the moorings below the lock and it is very noisy at night.

Typical narrow rock cut on the Trent-Severn Waterway.

Chart 2029, sheet 1 of 2.

Mile 212.7, Hamlet Swing Bridge (8'). Opens on demand.

Mile 214.0 to 240.7, Trent River. The next 26 miles are marked by numerous little lakes where the boater can leave the channel with ease and find a beautiful place to anchor without a problem.

Mile 213.8, Lauderdale Point Marina (705-689-2104,G,P). On the west shore in a protected basin this marina can handle larger transient vessels in 6'. 30A electric, showers, laundry and propane. Heavy weed growth was reported in 2006 and the current status is unknown.

Cruising The Trent-Severn Waterway, Georgian Bay, And North Channel
Chapter 8 – The Severn River

Mile 216.6, Deep Bay. At S212 head west and then southwest into Deep Bay for a great-protected anchorage. Feel your way across the 4 to 5 foot shoal at the entrance. Peaceful quiet anchoring abounds.

Mile 221.2, McDonald's Cut. Another one of these narrow rock lined cuts that took so long to make so this portion of the waterway would be navigable. Imagine excavating this cut by hand. No machinery in 1905.

Mile 224.5, Lock 43 Swift Rapids (47'). Really isolated and pristine. The only road in is 11 miles long, unpaved and very rough. This is a tall lock with a significant drop and is operated hydraulically. Above the lock there is overnight mooring [2] for 4 boats on the south wall with picnic tables and a great view of the spectacular generating plant out flow. Above the lock the blue line is on the north wall with room for 3 boats overnight. Although there is mooring below the lock, it is not recommended due to the swift currents and wakes from boats. Below the lock the blue line is on the north side with overnight mooring for 3-4 boats. There is also mooring room for 3 boats on the south wall.

Swift Rapids Hydro plant.

Mile 227.8, Severn Falls. The government dock on the west shore just before S138 provides deep-water dockage for vessels to 50' for a fee. 30A electric and water. It is an easy walk to a general store and restaurant.

Mile 230.5, Lost Channel. Turn north past S115 and explore this very picturesque waterway. Excellent anchoring in very clear and clean water. Explore to your hearts content, with water generally deep shore to shore except where indicated on your charts.

Chart 2029, Sheet 2 of 2.

Mile 232.5, Lock 44 Big Chute (57'). You are about to do something truly amazing. You will pilot your boat over land to the body of water below the pool at Big Chute. As you come into the basin at the topside of Big Chute, the long blue line is on the east shore (your port when headed to the Georgian Bay). It is NOT recommended that you tie up there, but go to one of the two piers in the center of the basin and tie up for a while. These two piers provide overnight mooring [2] for about 15 boats. Stopping here first will give you time to study the situation and the working of this railway lift.

Cruising The Trent-Severn Waterway, Georgian Bay, And North Channel
Chapter 8 – The Severn River

Near the center of the basin is the original small railway lift. Only 50 feet long it could carry only 18 tons and was generally limited to one large boat. It is no longer in service. To the east is the new visitors center and the larger railway lift. This larger lift can carry 110 tons and vessels up to 100' in length. More importantly, with its complex system of straps and rams it can carry a combination of boats up and down on each trip.

Big Chute Marina (705-756-2641,G,P) is located on the west shore (careful, you are headed south now if bound for the Georgian Bay) in the pool at Big Chute. Several larger transient vessels can be accomodated there. 30A electric, showers, and limited grocery items.

Loading the railcar at Big Chute.

Other than the marina and the visitor center there are no other services in the area.

Caution, it is **important** that you note the cross current at the top of the lift that flows to the east just in front of the railway car when it is submerged. Watch a couple of boats go into the railcar so you can appreciate how the current pulls boats to the port as they line up on the railway lift. If you approach the railway lift straight on but off center to starboard, the current will line you up for a smooth safe entry on the car just as you arrive there. You must know your boat to do this gracefully.

When you have spent as much time as you want at Big Chute, taking pictures and sightseeing, move over to the blue line and tie off. As the Parks Canada staff loads boats, they will give instructions over a loudspeaker. The first boat on the blue line is not always the first one called. Have bow and stern lines ready on both sides in the event they are needed, and have your sling positions marked so the staff can see them.

At the lower side (south) of the railway lift the long blue line is again on the east side. There is one floating dock on the west side with room for

Going over the top at Big Chute.

about 10 boats to tie up overnight [2]. However there is no easy access to shore from this dock. A second dock is attached to shore with room for about 5-6 boats, making access to shore much easier.

Traveling away from the Georgian Bay it is easier to enter the railway lift because there is no offsetting current below the lock.

Cruising The Trent-Severn Waterway, Georgian Bay, And North Channel
Chapter 8 – The Severn River

Mile 233.4, Little Chute. **Caution,** the Little Chute channel is narrow, the walls rocky and unforgiving and the current swift. Vessels down bound have the right away, but do not expect up bound vessels to know this or act accordingly. The down bound vessel should announce their presence on VHF-16 to alert any up bound vessels.

Mile 234 to 237, Gloucester Pool. A nice place to anchor and go ashore. The areas with circled red "Cs" or picnic table are public land. Unfortunately there are no docks here, but you can anchor and dinghy ashore.

Mile 234.1, O'Hara Point Marina Park (705-756-2284). One quarter mile NW of S80 in O'Hara Bay. Room for several larger transient vessels with 5' alongside. 30A electric, showers and laundry. A bakery nearby delivers fresh baked goods on order each morning.

Mile 234.5, Whites Falls Marina (705-756-2525,G,D,P). 1½ miles north of Wigwam Island in Whites Bay on the north shore. (1st of two marinas shown on the charts.) Room for several larger transient vessels alongside with 5' depth. 30A electric, and showers. Convenience store onsite.

Mile 238.5, The Narrows. **Caution,** the last of the narrow rocky channels. Stay alert at this point and follow your charts.

As you approach the Port Severn Lock there are five marinas in the immediate surrounding area.

    Severn Marina (705-538-2571, G,P), on the west shore. Vessels up to 40', reported depth is 5', 15A electric, showers.

    Driftwood Cove Resort Marina (705-538-2502, P), on the west shore. Vessels up to 50', reported depth 4', 30A electric, showers and internet.

    Severn Boat Haven (705-538-2975, G,D,P), on the east shore. Vessels up to 65', reported depth 6', 30A electric, showers and internet.

    Bush's Marine (705-538-2378, G), on the east shore. Vessels up to 48', reported depth 8', 30A electric, showers.

    Jim Earle Marine (866-JIM-EARLE, G) on east shore. Vessels up to 55', reported depth 5', 30A electric.

Mile 240.5, Lock 45 Port Severn (14') and Port Severn Road Swing Bridge (16'). This hand operated, extremely busy lock is the smallest lock in the system. Just beyond the lock, a swing bridge (16' closed vertical clearance) operates in conjunction with the lock schedule. The small resort town of Port Severn has some facilities and several of the marinas have restaurants.. Above the lock the blue line is on the east wall. There is overnight mooring [2] for four vessels on the dock extending out from the shore. There is also room for an additional 6 boats along the shore retaining wall on either side of that

Do Not Use For Navigation
Page - 48

Cruising The Trent-Severn Waterway, Georgian Bay, And North Channel
Chapter 8 – The Severn River

dock. Below the lock overnight mooring is available on the west side for 2 boats next to the park. The blue line below the lock is on the east wall.

Note: When leaving the lock bound for Georgian Bay, be mindful of the current as you approach the highway bridge. Normally the river flows at about 1 knot. During spring runoff the waters of the Severn River near mile 241 may flow at 3-4 knots. The channel here is marked with more than 10 buoys in rapid succession. Keep a constant speed so as not to lower your stern. Depths are dependent on the winds of Georgian Bay which can add or subtract a foot of depth to the already minimally deep channel.

Vessels northbound have completed the Trent-Severn Waterway and are ready to proceed to the Georgian Bay, Chapter 8. For vessels southbound, be sure to read chapter 3 before returning to chapter 8 at mile 240.5 above.

Cruising The Trent-Severn Waterway, Georgian Bay, And North Channel

Chapter 9
The Georgian Bay

The most striking feature of the Georgian Bay is its topography. Land both above and below water consists mostly of granite outcroppings. The surface of the many islands is a very thin soil over hard rock. Rugged pristine landscape abounds. On the southwest corner the shoreline of Bruce Peninsula is very steep and rocky. Close to shore the water is deep. There are few islands near the Bruce Peninsula and it is not an area that is recommended for the cruiser.

The northeast corner is quite the opposite. Blessed with numerous islands, the area provides many protected anchorages and channels that afford protection from strong winds when underway. This area is often referred to as the 30,000 islands. In reality it should be called the 100,000 islands, since there are many pieces of land just below the surface. While the channels are well marked and charted there are also many areas of the Georgian Bay that have never been charted. When traveling out of the channel having a bow lookout is a must. For a slow vessel the clear water allows for ample warning of submerged danger.

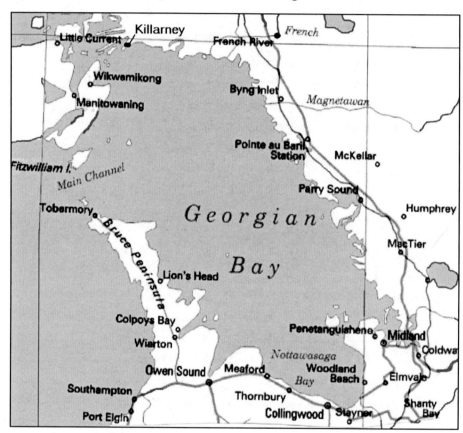

The Georgian Bay offers such a variety of cruising; with so many destinations and anchorages that one book cannot do it justice. Instead of covering all the Georgian Bay, we will simply cover the small craft route from Port Severn to Killarney along the northern edge of the Georgian Bay. This 168.5-mile trip offers the cruiser an opportunity to see every type of scenery the bay has to offer without ever having to cross a large open body of water. The small craft channel can easily handle a 50' vessel drawing 5-6'. There are a number of interesting ports to visit and literally millions of wonderful anchorages.

Weather

Weather reports are broadcast on VHF frequencies on both the weather channels and VHF 22 during the US Coast Guard update every 6 hours. In addition to any plain text broadcast, the VHF radio stations in the Great Lakes uses a system called MAFOR (Marine forecasting). This

Do Not Use For Navigation

Cruising The Trent-Severn Waterway, Georgian Bay, And North Channel
Chapter 9 – The Georgian Bay

is a coded five-digit number giving detailed weather information. The five digit number (XXXXX) gives the area of the forecast, number of hours, wind direction, wind speed (in knots) and weather conditions.

The first digit, Group ID, is usually 1 meaning the Great Lakes and this is usually preceded by the lake name in plain text. Example Lake Michigan 1XXXX. The second digit is the number of hours in the forecast period. X1XXX valid for 3 hours. The third digit is the wind direction. XX2XX wind east. The fourth number is the wind speed in knots. XXX3X wind 22-27. Finally the last number is weather condition. XXXX6 for rain. The complete MAFOR code table is shown below.

	No of Hours	Wind Dir	Wind Speed	Weather conditions
0	Now	Calm	0-10	Fine, mostly clear
1	3 hours	NE	11-16	Risk of ice
2	6 hours	E	17-21	Strong risk of ice
3	9 hours	SE	22-27	Mist, visibility to 3 miles
4	12 hours	S	28-33	Fog, visibility half mile or less
5	18 hours	SW	34-40	Drizzle
6	24 hours	W	41-47	Rain
7	48 hours	NW	48-55	Snow or rain/snow
8	72 hours	N	56-63	Squalls with/without showers
9	Sometimes	Variable	64-71	Thunderstorms

An example of a MAFOR whether forecast might be "Georgian Bay 13245". This would be interpreted as; "The weather on the Georgian Bay for the next 9 hours will be strong winds from the east at 28-33 knots with drizzle.

Charts

The following Charts are required to navigate the Small Craft Channel of the Georgian Bay: (See Appendix 1) The Small Craft Channel from Port Severn to the North Channel is indicated by a solid line on your charts. Dotted lines show alternative channels. Do to the large number of charts involved you may want to consider purchasing one of the commercially available chartbooks.

Canadian Hydrographic Charts 2202, 2203, 2204, 2245, 2251, 2257, 2259, 2286, 2299

NOAA Charts 14881, 14882

CAUTION: The Small Craft Channel has a designated depth of 6' at normal Lake Huron Chart Datum, 577.5 feet (176.022 meters). This is 1.9 to 2.6' above the Low Datum Level. This information is shown in the front of your chart kits. (Page ii) The depth of Lake Huron, and therefore the Georgian Bay varies throughout the year.

If Lake Huron drops in depth it may not be possible to carry a vessel of 6', or in some cases 5', draft through the entire Small Craft Channel. In these cases the boater will be required to

Cruising The Trent-Severn Waterway, Georgian Bay, And North Channel
Chapter 9 – The Georgian Bay

leave the Small Craft Channel and bypass part of the Small Craft Channel on the deeper Georgian Bay.

Current Lake Huron levels can be obtained at www.glerl.noaa.gov/data/now or call NOS at 301-713-9596. The levels will be given in meters. The Weather Radio also gives the lake levels during their routine broadcasts. Be sure to check to see what the Lake Huron level is with respect to Chart Datum during the period you are there. If the lake is 1' above Chart Datum you can add 1' to all charted depths. Likewise if the lake is 1' below Chart Datum, you must subtract 1' from all charted depths.

One final note on water depth. All of the Great Lakes as well as the Georgian Bay suffer a phenomena known as a "seiche". Think of it as a wind generated tide. When the wind blows in one direction for a prolonged period, the water tends to pile up on that end of the lake creating in effect a "high tide". Likewise, the water at the other end of the lake is blown away and you have a "low tide" there. Generally water level variation caused by strong consistent winds only amounts to a 1 or 2 foot variation in lake level. However, severe cases have been recorded over 5 feet. Keep this in mind when navigating and watch for unusual water depth changes not shown on the charts.

For those vessels in a hurry, you can depart Port Severn in the eastern end of the bay and head northwest to Killarney and by pass the entire small craft route. It is not recommend it since you will miss some of best and most beautiful cruising waters in North America.

Remember that marinas in Canada respond to VHF Channel 68, not 16. VHF 16 is to be used only for emergencies. Contact other vessels on VHF 09.

The small craft channel is well marked, but the prudent boater will keep a sharp lookout, proceed at slow speed and **STOP** the instant he is unsure of his location. In numerous locations there are rocks just below the surface outside the channel. In many places on your charts you will see large white areas marked "uncharted". It means just that. There is no guarantee that if you proceed into that area that you won't find a rock just a short way in. Where the charts are completed we have found them to be very accurate. However, even with good charts, once we left the channel we proceeded slowly with a bow lookout watching the water ahead of us. The water is very clear in the Georgian Bay and you normally can see the bottom in 10' of water. This should give most boaters ample warning of impending danger.

Caution: When anchoring in the Georgian Bay be sure to avoid submerged power lines (indicated by wiggly lines on your charts).

The remainder of this chapter is made up of highlights along the 168.5-mile rim route from Port Severn to Killarney. All points of interest are referenced by name and the statute mile marker shown on the small craft channel charts. The two best places to stock up on provisions in this stretch are Midland and Parry Sound.

Chart 2202.

Mile 0.0, Port Severn. When leaving Port Severn follow the main small craft channel behind Green Island. The main small craft channel is indicated on the small craft charts with a solid line. Alternate routes are shown in a dotted line.

Cruising The Trent-Severn Waterway, Georgian Bay, And North Channel
Chapter 9 – The Georgian Bay

Mile 5.2, Buoy BY. This is the point where you leave the small craft channel to head west-south-west for Midland, Georgian Bay's second largest town, with a population of 12,000. The downtown waterfront, close to the city's excellent shopping district, is the province of recreational boaters. Lake freighters are infrequent visitors, but a few times during the summer, large cruise ships from Europe will anchor out in the bay and several hundred visitors will come ashore via small craft. Do not approach these ships. In the wake of 9/11, it is not permitted, even in Canadian waters.

The Midland Harbour/ Town Dock (705-526-4610) offers transient space, water, electric, showers, a laundry, picnic tables and internet email. The transient rate for 2007 was $1.25/ft. Clients of the dockside restaurant may tie up free while dining.

Midland Marina (705-526-4433, G,P) is adjacent to the town dock and accepts transients. Electric service is 30A and there are washrooms with showers. A well stocked chandlery, Central Marine, is on site and a 15-ton hydraulic trailer is available for haul-out.

Across Midland Bay and opposite the Midland Town Docks is Bay Port Marina (705-527-7678, G,D,P). This is a new, massive facility that rivals any marina you have seen in the U.S. They offer transient dockage for vessels up to 100 feet, several restrooms with showers, laundry facilities, a pool and playground, on site ships store, a service yard with 50 ton haul out capability, mast stepping, internet email and much more.

Not far from Midland Bay is the Doral Marine Resort (1-866-253-6725, G,D,P). This facility is even larger than Bay Point and offers similar amenities and services. Transient rates for 2008 are $1.80/ft. with discounts for extended stays.

Midland offers all the services that a city of 12,000 needs, a great deal of it within walking distance of the town dock. In addition, there is an interesting historical museum, a reconstructed native Indian village, Marty's Shrine and Saint Marie Among the Hurons, a 17th century French settlement.

Mile 5.2, Buoy BY. Another great stop for historical purposes is just 9.6 miles by water west of Buoy BY and then south into Penetang Harbour. It is the village of Penetanguishene. **Note –** Anchoring is not permitted in Penetang Harbour. After entering the Penetang Harbour proceed to the entrance to the South Basin. On the west shore is the Port of Historic Penetanguishene. The Port of Historic Penetanquishene (P) provides transient dockage for larger vessels and provides 30A

Cruising among the many islands.

electric, showers and laundry. In addition, you can arrange to tie up at the visitors dock for short periods at no charge while shopping. Discovery Harbour is a reconstruction of a 19th century British naval base complete with soldiers and sailors dressed in the period. There are many historic buildings there, a boardwalk, theme shop, and tours of historic

Cruising The Trent-Severn Waterway, Georgian Bay, And North Channel
Chapter 9 – The Georgian Bay

buildings. Individuals dressed in the period carry on chores similar to Williamsburg in VA. A wonderfully educational stop showing the main British Naval Base on the Upper Great Lakes.

Within 10 minutes walk of the Port of Historic Penetanquishene you have the Beer Store, LCBO, pharmacy, bank (ATM), and IGA grocery as well as many restaurants and small shops.

Bay Moorings Yacht Club (705-549-6958,G,D,P) is on the east shore 0.8 miles north of Penetanquishene. They provide transient dockage for about 30 vessels up to 50' in deep water. 50A electric, shower and laundry. ($1.25/ft – 2006)

Beacon Bay Marina (705-549-2075,G,D,P) is in a basin at the southern end of South Basin. They provide transient dockage for larger vessels in 8' of water. 50A electric, showers, laundry, E-mail hookup, and swimming pool.

Hindson Marine (705-549-2991,G,D,P) is located at the southwest tip of South Basin and provides transient dockage for larger vessels in 6' of water. 50A electric, showers and swimming pool.

Note: As you cruise through the Georgian Bay and its 30,000 island and in the North Channel look for areas on land on your charts shaded in dark brown. This indicates public land. Not only can you go ashore here, you will often find some type of facilities there and even some docks. Your annual mooring pass is valid at these docks. A circled "C" or picnic table also indicates public landings.

Mile 11.2, Picnic Island Resort (705-756-2421,G,P). On the east side of the channel on Picnic Island this facility provides easy access for quick shopping. (No overnight) Water, charts and propane. Large selection of groceries.

Mile 11.4, Honey Harbour. Just to the east of the channel behind Picnic Island is the small tourist community of Honey Harbour. The town dock, in the bay northeast of Picnic Island, is a free two-hour shopping dock for boats up to 25 feet. Most boats there will be local cottagers' runabouts. There is only 3 feet of water in the slips and a fee is charged for staying overnight. Turn east just north of the red and green day markers to find your way in.

Paragon Marina (705-756-2402,G,P) is located on the tip of the peninsula as you enter the bay behind Picnic Island. Transient space for larger vessels in 6' of water with 50A electric, showers and email.

Honey Harbour provides grocery, hardware, post office, bank (ATM), and LCBO.

Mile 11.6, Beausoleil Island. Just to the west of C93 through the Big Dog Channel lies Beausoleil Island, one of the Parks Canada National Parks. This island offers several places where you can tie up to a dock and relax among the camaraderie of the Canadian boaters. If you purchased the Annual Mooring Pass to go through the Trent-Severn Canal, that pass is honored here. Stay a day, stay a week. **Note** – A couple of docks on Beausoleil Island are marked "reserved". If you elect to tie up there, there is a $10 fee in addition to your mooring pass. There are restrooms and picnic areas, but no power. The most popular and best-protected Parks Canada dock off Beausoleil Bay is in Ojibway Bay, on the east shore of Beausoleil Island. The dock in Ojibway Bay is isolated but has

Do Not Use For Navigation

Cruising The Trent-Severn Waterway, Georgian Bay, And North Channel
Chapter 9 – The Georgian Bay

access to the well marked trail system on the island. You can walk the full length of the island.

Further down near the south end of the east side of Beausoleil Island there are three docks between Finger Point and Papoose Bay. The middle dock is reserved for Parks Canada and handicapped personnel. Both of the other two docks allow overnight mooring. The advantage of these two docks is that they are closer to the visitor center. The disadvantage of these two docks is that the ferries dock at the Main Wharf (southern most dock) and their wake can be unpleasant.

You can also anchor in good protection in the northwest corner of Beausoleil Bay or closer to the visitor center just off the Main Wharf. Later on at mile 14.4 you will have another opportunity to tie up to Beausoleil Island in Frying Pan Bay, probably the most popular dock on Beausoleil Island.

From the east side of Beausoleil Island it is a short dinghy ride east through Big Dog Channel to the tourist community of Honey Harbour where you can purchase ice cream and other essentials at inflated prices.

Canadians like to come to their National Parks Islands and spend their vacation. Often 3 or 4 boats traveling together will tie up to one dock. Out comes the portable generator that they carry up into the woods. They operate the generator for all the boats in their group. Next the lawn chairs are brought out and they set up for the duration. Often this will be one or two weeks.

Med mooring on the Georgian Bay.

Mile 11.7, Delawana Inn Resort. On the east side of the channel on Picnic Island this resort provides transient space for larger vessels in 6' of water with easy access to Honey Harbour. No fuel.

Mile 12.0, South Bay. Off to the east lies the waterway leading to South Bay. There are many excellent anchorages along this route. As you go north on the small craft channel you will find many places where you can pull off the channel and sound your way in to a quiet bay to anchor for the night. Most often in the Georgian Bay the shore will be lined with summer cottages or homes. Most of the property is private and you should not go ashore unless invited. Frequently you can wind your way up one channel and then back another as you circumnavigate an island. If the bottom is rocky and you can't get the anchor to hold, just move to another bay. Don't forget the bow look out, go slowly, study your charts, and have a great time.

As you enter South Bay on your starboard are 4 marinas in a row. Only one offers transient space and can handle larger vessels in at least 8' of water. The second one, Admiral's Marina (705-756-2432,G,D,P), 30A electric, showers and E-mail hookup.

If you continue further up the Main Channel east you will find the large well equipped South Bay Cove Marina, (705-756-3333,G,D,P), 50A electric, free ice and newspaper. The chart to South Bay Cove Marina shows shallow water but it is on a deep-

Cruising The Trent-Severn Waterway, Georgian Bay, And North Channel
Chapter 9 – The Georgian Bay

water channel. South Bay Cove Marina is east of Honey Harbor beyond Lownie Island in the protected cove at N44° 52.11 and W79° 46.84.

Mile 14.4, Beausoleil Island. Frying Pan Bay offers another great place to tie up on Beausoleil Island and use your mooring pass. This is the most isolated park dock on Beausoleil Island, but also one of the most popular.

Mile 15 to 17, Musquash Channel and Bone Island. A number of quiet and protected anchorages are available off the small craft channel to the NE. One of the easier protected anchorages can be found in the long unnamed fjord like bay at the NW end of Bone Island. While there are no submerged power lines here, it is surrounded by private land and there is nowhere to land. There is a fairly protected bay on the south center side of Bone Island, but the approach is much more difficult. However, there is public land there where you can go ashore and as well as anchoring, there is Parks Canada dockage there.

Mile 20 to 27. The channel is rather exposed to the southwest here and that is the direction of the prevalent winds. For more protection you can leave the small craft channel at C116 and proceed behind Galbraith Island via Monument Channel following the alternate dotted red line channel. If the winds are still too strong pick a spot to anchor in North Go Home Bay. Rejoin the main small craft channel at C127.

Mile 26.2, Indian Harbour. Follow the alternate route behind Bands Island to anchor in Indian Harbour. Holding is difficult due to the rocky bottom, but many boaters like the convenience of this spot. Private land surrounds the harbour, so you cannot go ashore.

Mile 34.0, O'Donnel Point. Note the three islands adjacent to the channel shaded a darker brown. These are National Parks Islands (without docks) where you can freely go ashore. Also at mile 34.7, can C154 you can turn east up Twelve Mile Bay and you will find a large piece of the south shoreline between Bowes Island and Moose Point Indian Reserve set aside as National Parks territory. Here again you can feel free to go ashore.

    The water is deep to the bank and the most common mooring here is the "Med Mooring". You tie your stern to a tree on shore and anchor your bow out about 100' from shore. This way you can get close to shore and still not have to worry about your boat drifting into the shoreline if the wind shifts. You will find the Med Mooring used extensively in the North Channel and Georgian Bay in small-protected harbors.

Mile 34.5 to 40.0. To the east of the channel are hundreds of channels and bays to explore. If you have time on your hand use the charts to work your way east to Moon, Port Rawson, or Spider Bay.

Mile 40.1, LeBlanc's Sans Souci Marina (705-746-5598,G,D,P). No transient space, but food and fuel. Just past C179 turn west and follow the channel into the marina. 4' alongside with groceries and LCBO/Beer Store.

Mile 40.5, Fryingpan Island. OK so you aren't totally lost. On the north shore of Fryingpan Island is an excellent restaurant at Sans Souci. Henry's Fish Restaurant (G) provides a

Cruising The Trent-Severn Waterway, Georgian Bay, And North Channel
Chapter 9 – The Georgian Bay

first class meal at a reasonable price. There is also dockage there for more than 40 boats. Be sure to call ahead on VHF channel 68 for docking instructions. 30A electric and showers.

Mile 41.8, Echo Bay. For a protected anchorage try Echo Bay. Past C183 and west of Ajax Island turn west to the opening between Echo Island and Sans Souci Island. The entrance to north Echo Bay is shallow (5') and rocky so approach with caution. Once inside the water is deep (>25') with good holding. The shoreline is part of Massasauga Provincial Park with walking trails. Dinghy about 2 miles to Henry's Fish Restaurant.

Mile 42.3, South Channel. If northbound, now is the time to decide if you want to visit the community of Parry Sound. By far the largest community on the Georgian Bay, it is located 14 miles up the South Channel. To bypass Parry Sound continue on the Small Craft Channel.
    To visit Parry Sound continue on the South Channel route.

By-passing the South Channel and Parry Sound.

Mile 51.3, Hale Bay. If you are not visiting Parry Sound you will find a good anchorage to the west of the Small Craft Channel. As you pass CS15 northbound, Sandy Island is to your west. Continue another mile and then turn west proceeding into Hale Bay on Sandy Island passing between Ross Point and Allen Island. Anchor where space permits in 15' with good holding. Quiet protected anchorage with only a few houses. Continue on the main route until you rejoin the channel from Parry Sound west of Rose Island.

Taking the South Channel to Parry Sound.

Mile 46.1, Redner Bay. One of many fine anchorages along the South Channel. Redner Bay is on the east shore. Remember that most of the adjoining land is private and you should not go ashore.

Mile 47.7, Kineras Bay. On the south shore, larger and more exposed than Redner Bay, but still popular as an anchorage.

Mile 50.8, Five Mile Bay. Large bay to SW from the channel that offers many smaller bays where you can anchor.

Mile 51.3, Dunroe Island. Anchor on the east side of Dunroe Island for protection from passing wakes.

Mile 53.8, Rose Point railroad bridge (18'). Actually an automobile bridge that opens only on the hour between 6AM and 10PM.

Mile 55.8, Parry Sound. Parry Sound is roughly six miles long by six miles wide. Here, beyond the town, the scenery takes on a softer aspect as trees cover the rock more generously than on the outer shores and islands. This is the best place to provision between southern

Cruising The Trent-Severn Waterway, Georgian Bay, And North Channel
Chapter 9 – The Georgian Bay

Georgian Bay and Little Current. When approaching the harbor be alert for floatplanes. There are frequent flights in and out and it is not unusual to see a floatplane maneuvering next to you. The Town Dock is a long concrete dock jutting out into Parry Sound Harbor (P). There is ample dockage on both sides with 30A electric and showers. This dock is very busy on weekends. On Sequin Street you will find a supermarket, bakery, LCBO, and hardware. Within 3 blocks there are restaurants, several banks, Laundromat, the Beer Store, and an A&P supermarket.

Big Sound Marina (705-746-4213, P, WiFi) is located in the inner harbor. Transient dockage up to 60' with 30A electric and showers. The transient rate for 2008 is $1.25/ft.

Parry Sound Marine (705-746-5848,G,D,P) is located to the east side of the harbor opposite the Public Pier. Room for a few transient vessels with 30A electric and washrooms.

Pier 99 Marina (705-746-8222) is located on the east side of the harbor just south of Parry Sound Marine. Room for a number of larger transient vessels. 50A electric, cable TV, and showers.

The Sound Boat Works (705-746-2411,G,D,P) is ½ mile south on the east shore near the range lights. There is room for a few larger transient vessels. 30A electric and showers.

Point Pleasant Marina (705-746-9671,G,P) is 1 mile south on the east shore near Jenkins Point. There is room for several transient vessels up to 36'. 30A electric and showers.

Note - To rejoin the small craft channel head west out Parry Sound 10.0 miles and past Killbear Point to your north to rejoin the small craft channel at mile 10.0. Killbear Marina (705-342-5203, G,D,P) is located in Pengallie Bay. Electric is 30A, showers, and a well stocked ships store. Can accommodate vessels up to 60'

Chart 2203.

Mile 10.0, Parry Sound. The statute mile markers start over on map **page 146** at 0 at Parry Sound. Mile 55.0 becomes 10.0.

Mile 13.0, Canoe Channel. **Caution,** the small craft channel passes behind Squaw Island at mile 13.6. Canoe Channel is so narrow that it is not considered suitable for vessels over 40'. Larger vessels should go around Squaw Island to the south and rejoin the small craft channel at mile 14.5 just beyond PJ5-PJ6.

Mile 15.7, Snug Harbour. Snug Harbour lies one mile to the east of the small craft channel between Snug Island and Middle Island. The public dock is on the port side just before Snug Harbour Marine. There is a small convenience store there and Gilly's Restaurant, with gas and a pumpout, but not much else.

Some vessels anchor near the entrance to Snug Harbour north of the channel and east of Westyle Island in 18-20' with good holding. Dinghy into Snug Harbour for supplies or to eat in the restaurant.

Cruising The Trent-Severn Waterway, Georgian Bay, And North Channel
Chapter 9 – The Georgian Bay

Mile 16.7, Regatta Bay. West of the channel via a marked channel lies the popular Franklin Island anchorage. Caution only 4' water at the entrance. Good holding. A popular spot with picnic tables and a floating dock for a couple of boats.

Mile 20.0, Narrows Island. Off to the north and east are Sand, Shebeshekong, and Long Bays. Notice there are no charted depths. **Caution,** if you decide to go in here remember your bow lookout and go slow.

Mile 22.9, Jack Island. Off to south a semi-protected anchorage can be found between Jack and Haggart Islands.

Mile 25.0, Shawanaga Inlet. You will notice a lot of uncharted bays as you proceed east from here. Many of them are deep enough for you to explore. Just remember to go slow and post a look out.

Mile 30.2, Shawanaga Inlet. Note the alternate channel to the northeast that ultimately rejoins the main small craft channel at mile 35.4. You should take this channel if you wish to visit Point Au Baril Station. Turn to **Page 138.**
   Tonches Island. At Marjorie Point on Tonches Island turn to the north and then east and head up Brignall Banks Narrows 3 miles to the well protected Point Au Baril Station.
   One and a half miles up Brignall Banks Narrows (half way to Point Au Baril Stations) on the starboard side on Ontario Banks is Payne Marine Ltd (705-366-2296,G,P), the only marina in the area large enough to accommodate larger vessels.

   At Point Au Baril Station, two public docks serve the visiting boater. One is a long wooden dock sticking out into the harbor. The other is a concrete pier on your starboard as you approach the small community. CC Kennedy Co. provides a general store there with groceries and most everything else. A few blocks away is Highway 69 with another grocery, the Beer Store, and LCBO. There are no banks, pharmacies or Laundromats in Point Au Baril.

Point Au Baril Lighthouse

Mile 35.4, Point Au Baril channel. Leaving Point Au Baril Station, rejoin the small craft channel here. If east bound depart the small craft channel here for Point Au Baril Station.

Do Not Use For Navigation

Cruising The Trent-Severn Waterway, Georgian Bay, And North Channel
Chapter 9 – The Georgian Bay

Mile 37.2, Buoy RGR. **Caution,** do not cut buoy RGR short. Go around it and turn to the northeast.

Caution: In years of low water, the small craft channel from 37.2 to 47.0 is recommended only for vessels of 5' draft or less. If your vessel draws more than 5' proceed out into the Georgian Bay at Buoy RGR and rejoin the small craft channel after mile 47.0.

Mile 40.4, Hangdog Reef. **Caution,** do not cut buoy A74 short. Go around it and turn to the northeast.

Mile 43.4, Bayfield Harbour. If winds are acting up on the Georgian Bay there are many places you can anchor and wait out the weather in Bayfield Harbour. In addition, there are two marinas:

Hangdog Marina (705-366-2000) is located 0.7 miles up Bayfield Harbour on the north shore where the chart indicates Georgian Inlet. Room for several large vessels with 6' alongside this marina does not monitor VHF. No electric or fuel.

Thompson Marine (705-366-2235,G,D) is located 1.3 miles up Bayfield Harbour on the north shore where the chart indicates Bayfield Inlet. Room for 5 large vessels with 6' alongside, VHF 68. 30A electric, and showers.

Mile 47 to 55. This stretch past the Head Islands is rather open to the west and not pleasant in a strong southwest wind. There are places to get in off the channel, but they are not marked with buoys and this is not a good place to go exploring in strong winds.

Mile 52.2. Georgian Bay, Norgate Rocks. **Caution:** The channel shown on Canadian Chart 2203, Sheet 3 of 3 has been moved. The small craft channel is shown on existing charts as passing east of Norgate Rocks using buoys A118 to A127. The channel and buoys have been moved west of Norgate Rocks. The same buoy numbers are used and the channel is well marked.

Mile 57.5, South Channel. Unless you are going east to Byng Inlet, you curve to the north at H21 and take A149 and A151 on your port side. You join the new small craft channel at mile 58.5, which is mile 4.7 of the next chart at D2.

Mile 61.0, Wright's Marina (705-383-2295,G,D,P). On the north shore before Old Mill Island. Room for several large transient vessels in more than 8' of water. 30A electric.

Mile 62.0, St Amant's Waterfront Inn and Marina (705-383-2434,G,D,P). On the north shore midway between H47 and H49. Room for more than 30 large transient vessels with 6' of water. 30A electric, shower and laundry.

Mile 62.5, Buisson's Food Market. On the north shore at the mouth of the Still River provides a large shopping dock alongside with 8' of water. Complete selection of groceries and other essentials. LCBO/Beer store inside and post office near by.

Do Not Use For Navigation

Cruising The Trent-Severn Waterway, Georgian Bay, And North Channel
Chapter 9 – The Georgian Bay

Chart 2204.

Mile 4.7, North Channel. The chart starts over with new numbers on this chart and you join the small craft channel at mile 4.7.

Mile 8.0 to 13.0. Lots of uncharted waters to the east of the channel. Great place to explore on a calm day. Not good under pressure in windy conditions.

Mile 8.8, Sandy Bay. Good anchorage in long finger of white charted on the south side of Sandy Bay. Feel your way in.

Mile 12.4, Rogers Island. Good anchorage in white-charted area just south of Rogers Island. Feel your way in. White painted stakes imbedded into the top of the vertical rock face make it easy to tie up alongside the wall. 6' alongside at normal chart datum except at the east end which has only 3'.

Mile 17.7, Dead Island. Semi protected anchorage in 10' east of Dead Island.

Mile 18.7, RGR. If you want to avoid crossing the Northeast Passage you can follow the alternative small craft channel behind the Outer Fox Islands. Otherwise, follow the main small craft channel across the Northeast Passage. If the weather forecast is not good, the alternative channel gives you ample places to wait before it rejoins the main small craft channel at mile 25.2.

Mile 22.2, Tie Island. Leave the channel before D70 and proceed through the deep-water channel behind Northeast and Tie Island. Anchor in this well protected spot in 10-12'.

Mile 23.7, The Gun Barrel. Depart the channel at D78 and follow the alternate channel south into The Gun Barrel. Feel your way south and pick a spot between Pearl and Green Island for a protected anchorage in 12'.

Mile 25.2 to 42.0, Lake Huron. This is the most exposed portion of the trip up the Georgian Bay. Although there are lots of places to hide just to the north of the channel, there are no marked entrances and lots of dangerous rocks. This is not the area where you want to be looking for a place to hide in strong winds and rough seas.

Caution: From mile 46.5 to 47.0 the water can be very shallow, particularly if Lake Huron is low. During periods of low water (below chart datum) deep draft vessels may have to bypass the safety of the Collins Inlet passage and take the unprotected 20-mile route on Lake Huron. Depart the small craft channel at mile 40.1 and head for Killarney Channel mile 64.0 staying in deep water.

Mile 43.0 to 59.5, Collins Inlet. These few miles are some of the most protected and pristine on the trip up the Georgian Bay. The rock formations really belong in the North Channel.

Do Not Use For Navigation

Cruising The Trent-Severn Waterway, Georgian Bay, And North Channel
Chapter 9 – The Georgian Bay

Mile 43.0, Burnt Island. Follow the shoreline heading almost due north at MacFarlane Island to work your way up behind Burnt Island. Nice anchorage except in W to N winds.

Mile 51.0, Crabby Indian. Just after you enter Collins Inlet northbound look for the profile of the face of the crabby Indian on the north shore (your starboard).

Mile 57.2, Collins Inlet. Leave the channel north of Keyhole Island and follow the north shore behind the island on the chart with no name. Anchor in 10-15' is this protected spot.

Mile 65.0, Killarney. After 168.5 miles the trip from Port Severn to Killarney is over.

Cruising The Trent Severn Canal, Georgian Bay, And North Channel

Chapter 10
The North Channel

The North Channel provides protected passage between Manitoulin Island and Ontario's southern shore. Technically, Killarney is part of Georgian Bay. It is however, a natural place to begin your journey of this impressive area. For purposes of this book the North Channel lies nearly east west and runs from Killarney in the east to De Tour Village in the west, 138 statute miles.

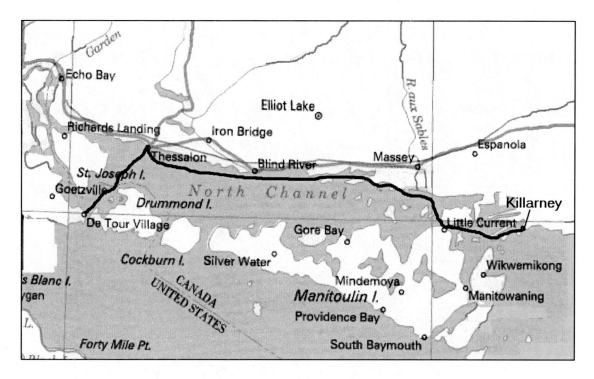

Created by glaciers in the not too distant past, while geologically young, the North Channel has some of the oldest rocks in the world exposed on its north shore. Many of the rocks in this area are more than 3 billion years old. The shoreline is rugged and sparsely populated. Because of this cruisers can anchor out (med mooring style) and go ashore in many locations.

The remainder of this chapter, we will lead you through the North Channel by the most direct and safest route to De Tour Village on upper Lake Huron. We will also include some interesting side trips and wonderful anchorages. If you have time, enjoy this wonderful, primitive cruising area.

You may wish to mark off your charts in statute miles as all points of interest will be identified by both the mile marker and chart name for ease of reference.

The small craft channel across the North Channel is not marked on your charts. The channel day marks are on the chart, but there is no solid or dashed line leading you across each chart. To make matters worse, you will switch back and forth between different scale charts, many overlapping one another. It is a good idea to study your charts of the North Channel before starting. Further, consider marking the "small craft channel" of the North Channel on your charts using a yellow or pink "high light" marker.

Do Not Use For Navigation

Cruising The Trent-Severn Waterway, Georgian Bay, And North Channel
Chapter 10 – The North Channel

What follows is the mile-by-mile description of your passage up the North Channel.

Chart 2245.

Mile 0.4, Killarney. On the north shore this small community provides a great stop for cruisers. In addition to several marinas (see below), you can tie up to one of three other places, all on the north shore.

First is Pitfield's General Store with groceries. You can tie up, room permitting, and stock up. Pitfield's is the only place to stock up with groceries in Killarney.

The next dock west is the LCBO and Beer Store. Yes, you can pull up to the dock and stock up with liquor if you wish.

Finally, there is Herbert Fisheries and there is room for 2 boats on the outside of the dock and a few small boats inside the dock. Check in with Herbert Fisheries store. A bus selling fried-fish is on the premises. You can walk to the essential places in town. No bank in Killarney, but there is a bakery, Laundromat, souvenir shop and several restaurants.

Killarney Mountain Lodge (800-461-1117,G,D,P) is the first marina on the north shore you encounter in Killarney when west bound. With a depth of 6' at the docks and room for more than 30 large transient boats, this marina provides 50A electric, and showers.

Gateway Marine and Storage (705-287-2333,P) is the next marina on the north shore beyond the public dock. Room for 15 larger transient vessels in 6'. 30A electric, showers and laundry.

Sportsman's Inn. This facility was not operational during 2007. As of March 2008 there was no information available regarding its status for 2008. A telephone call to the Municipal Offices in Killarney and a real estate agent confirmed that the property had been sold in late 2007.

Rogue's Marina (705-287-9900) is the last marina on the north shore. There is room for several larger transient vessels in 5' of water. 30A electric and showers.

Mile 1.5, Covered Portage Cove. For one of those wonderful protected anchorages, turn north between E6-E8 and head up past Sheep Island, favoring the island side and into Killarney Bay. On the east bank is Covered Portage Cove. Proceed all the way in to find deeper water than charted. A favorite among boaters, expect to find company in there for the night, anchored med mooring style in the clear water. Good idea to use a trip line both to ease recovery of your anchor and allow later arrivals to see where your anchor is.

Mile 2.8, Snug Harbor. Another great anchorage awaits you north of Badgeley Island. Midway along Badgeley Point on the north shore is Snug Harbor. The entrance will carry 5', but proceed slowly and favor the centerline. Once inside the deep quiet pool you will find lots of company to share this great protected anchorage.

Mile 12.0, Baie Fine. Once well past the west end of Partridge Island head north to a unique experience on Baie Fine. Probably the closest thing to a fjord you will ever cruise in. The entrance is six miles north of the small craft channel. For a wonderful experience,

Do Not Use For Navigation

Cruising The Trent-Severn Waterway, Georgian Bay, And North Channel
Chapter 10 – The North Channel

cruise the entire 10 miles of the bay to The Pool at the end. There is great blueberry picking on the north shore above The Pool.

Many vessels stop after 2 miles and enter Mary Ann Cove on the south bank. The chart shows an island there and you cannot go around the island, as it is too shallow. Enter on the west side and anchor med mooring style in the company of 8-10 boats. The hills above Mary Ann Cove are great to climb and the view of Frazer Bay is breath taking from Frazer Bay Hill. There are also many blueberry bushes on the hillside. Expect blueberry pancakes, muffins, etc. for several days after a visit here.

Mary Ann Cove in Bay Fine

Chart 2286 Caution: Depths shown on this chart are in fathoms.

Mile 23.8, Harbour View Marina (705-368-3212,G,P), Little Current. On the south shore near J27 just before you enter the cut at Little Current. Room for more several transient vessels in 8' of water. 30A electric, and showers.

Mile 24.5, railroad swing bridge (18') Goat Island Channel. **Restricted:** Opens only on the hour for up to 15 minutes for pleasure craft, unless a train is coming. **Caution,** there is often a surprising amount of current flowing under the bridge. After months with no tidal current this may catch you by surprise. The current is wind driven and may flow in either direction at up to 4 knots at the bridge.

Mile 25.0, Little Current. Located on the south shore on Manitoulin Island in a narrow channel between Manitoulin and Goat Island. The 1500' town dock (G,D,P) is along the south shore about ½ mile beyond the bridge. The dock can get crowded and rafting is expected. **Caution,** take the current into account when docking. While not as strong as under the bridge, it still must be taken into account when docking; especially if trying to raft with a strangers new sailboat. At the east end of the town docks are showers.

Note – From July to August the Little Current Cruisers Network broadcasts on VHF 71 at 9AM providing marine weather, news, community events, and relaying messages.

Within three blocks you can find Dunn's Freshmart (supermarket), hardware store, pharmacy, banks (ATM), ice cream store, Foodmart Bakery and Deli, LCBO and Beer Store. Who could ask for more? There are of course numerous fast food and restaurants.

At the west end of the town dock is Boyle Marine (705-368-2239). Room for 6 large transient vessels in 6' of water. 30A electric and showers.

Spider Bay Marina (705-368-3148,G,D,P) is the last marina on the south shore as you go through the cut at Little Current. Can accommodate vessels up to 70' in 6' of water. 50A electric, showers, laundry and propane.

Anglican Church at Kagawong.

Mile 27.5, Sturgeon Bay. If you are looking for a quiet secluded and protected anchorage try Sturgeon Bay. Located at N46° 02.8 and W81° 51.5 on the north side of Great La Cloche Island. West bound as you break out of the narrows at Little Current turn to the north and work your way up between East Rous Island and Great La Cloche Island. Follow the deep-charted water to the north and then east around Great La Cloche Island to the entrance to Sturgeon Bay. Use a lookout and work your way into the protected bay with a mud bottom and great protection. Isolated and serene.

Chart 2299. Used primarily to get to Kagawong or Clapperton Island.

Mile 33.9, Clapperton Island. There is an excellent anchorage on the south side of Clapperton Island marked as Clapperton Harbour. Depart the small ship channel south of Amedroz Island and work your way south and west into Clapperton Channel (see map 103 and 104 as well). At about W82° 15 head generally north into the protected harbor charted as Clapperton Harbour at N46° 00 and W82° 14. Good depth, mud bottom and great protection from most winds.

Mile 34.0, Kagawong. A 10-mile side trip south of Clapperton Island to the small community of Kagawong provides two interesting sights. Bridal Veil Falls and the Anglican Church. Both worth a visit. Round Bedford Island to the south. Clear James Foote Patch on your starboard and head for Clapperton Channel. Round Gooseberry Island and head south-southwest into Mudge Bay. At the bottom of Mudge Bay is Kagawong.

There is transient dockage at the Northern Marina in Kagawong, and a public dock. Anchor off, go to the marina or tie up at the public dock. The Angelican Church is located near the public dock and is adorned with parts from boats. It is interesting to see. A short walk from town along the designated path brings you to Bridal Veil Falls (about ½ mile). You can swim in the pool at the base of the falls, walk behind the falls or just enjoy the cool air from the falls. On a hot summer day it is about 10 degrees cooler at the base of the falls.

Cruising The Trent-Severn Waterway, Georgian Bay, And North Channel
Chapter 10 – The North Channel

Kagawong offers a general store with groceries, LCBO/Beer Store and post office all in one store less than a block from the public dock.

Northern Marina (705-282-3330,G,P) of Kagawong adjacent to the town dock provides room for about 10 large transient vessels in 6'. 30A electric and showers.

Bridal Veil Falls at Kagawong.

Mile 39.0, Benjamin Islands. A group of islands referred to as the Benjamin Islands is located north of Clapperton Island. The best anchorage in the Benjamin Islands is on Croker Island and is approached from the south. Whether coming from Kagawong or the small craft channel head for a point north of Clapperton Island in the Main Passage. South of Croker Island head west and pass Wilson Point and then Secretary Island before turning north and working your way into the protected bay in the bottom west side of Croker Island. Great blueberries and interesting view from Wilson Point. When leaving head east around the south end of Croker Island and proceed far enough east to join the channel half way between U8 and U9.

Chart 2257.

Mile 45.7, Anchor Island. North of Fox Island there is a quiet protected anchorage in 8' between Anchor Island and the mainland. It is private land, so no going ashore. Feel your way in to this anchorage and use a bow lookout.

Mile 47.9, Eagle Island. Not as protected, Eagle Island provides good protection for all but a northeast wind. Proceed south below Frechette Island and anchor in the cove on the north shore of Eagle Island in 6'.

Mile 50.6, Hotham Island. Several good anchorages in the water north of Hotham Island. Enter via the channel between Oak Point and the west end of Hotham Island. Not as narrow as the chart makes it look. Keep a bow lookout and feel your way into the best cove for protection from the prevailing wind.

Mile 54.3, Little Detroit Strait. **Caution,** this channel requires special caution because it is so narrow. It is common practice to announce your intentions to pass on VHF Channel 16 before entering this strait.

Do Not Use For Navigation

Cruising The Trent-Severn Waterway, Georgian Bay, And North Channel
Chapter 10 – The North Channel

Mile 54.8, Spanish. **Caution:** The entrance channel to Spanish often shoals in. Call ahead to the Spanish Marina before trying the entrance to the channel at UV1 and UV2 or feel your way in.

    If you want to go to Spanish, just after departing Little Detroit Strait turn north and pass Green Island on your port. Continue north leaving the two black day marks on your port also. Between Whiteaves and Fletcher Islands you can see the channel markers for the Spanish Channel. Follow the 6' deep channel east and the public dock will be the first dock on your port. Three marinas are located just a little further east.

    In Spanish a half-mile walk north brings you to Front Street, Spanish's main street. Located there you will find grocery stores, hardware, pharmacy, banks, the LCBO and Beer Store. There are a number of good restaurants and fast food places within walking distance on Front Street.

    On approaching Spanish the first marina on port is the Spanish Municipal Marina (705-844-1077,G,D,P). Room for more than 70 larger transient vessels in 5'. 50A electric, showers and laundry.

    When departing northbound, head west out the channel and then southwest between Thomas and Gervase Islands to join the small craft channel one half mile north of U15.

Mile 56.2, Jackson Island. Leave the channel WSW behind Passage, Villiers, and Otter Islands to anchor in deep water between Jackson and Aird Island.

Chart 2259.

Mile 67.9, John Island. Leave the channel south at Turtle Rock U27 and proceed around the west end of Gowan Island. Follow the deep water easterly between Dewdney and John Island to anchor in 6' near the end of the channel in John Harbor.

Mile 71.5, Prendergast Island. The North Channel Yacht Club (705-849-9052,G,D,P) lies to the north east of this island in Serpent Harbor. Round Prendergast Island and bear north past Navy island, then northeast past the lime plant toward Meteor Rock. Follow the channel into Serpent Harbor to the North Channel Yacht Club.

Mile 77.5, Sanford Island. At this point the small craft channel proceeds out into the open waters of the North Channel. From here to Thessalon, mile 114.0, the water is exposed and should be traversed only on a good day. Pick your weather carefully.

Mile 82.0, Blind River. Head northwest from the small craft channel and pass UP2 on your starboard. The enclosed basin (Blind River Marine Park) for small craft is ½ mile to the west of the Blind River Bridge. About where the "WT" is shown on your chart. No place to anchor, but there is a marina here and town is about a one mile walk north and east across the bridge. On the main street of town, Causley Street, there is a grocery, restaurants, the Beer Store, pharmacy, movie theater, and banks. The LCBO is two blocks north on Woodward Ave.

    Blind River Marine Park (705-356-7026,G,D,P) provides transient space for larger vessels in 6'. 30A electric, showers and laundry and internet.

Do Not Use For Navigation

Cruising The Trent-Severn Waterway, Georgian Bay, And North Channel
Chapter 10 – The North Channel

Charts 2299, 2251.

Mile 114.0, Thessalon. The small craft channel stays off the northern shore 2-3 miles and heads generally west passing the East Grant Island on your south or port. There are good anchorages in East Grant and West Grant Islands. After approaching Thessalon Point follow the small craft channel up the east side of Thessalon Point to the Thessalon Marina. There is room to anchor north of the breakwater east of KA2. It is a fair anchorage in terms of wind protection.

Two blocks north of the marina on Main Street you will find a grocery store, bakery, LCBO/ Beer Store, hardware store, banks (ATM), and pharmacy. This is a good place to change your Canadian Money back to US once all your expenses are accounted for.

Thessalon Marina (705-842-5188,G,D,P) provides space for 15 larger transient vessels in 6'. 30A electric, and showers.

If stopping here, pick your weather before continuing on to De Tour Village. Also note, you can continue west here up the St Joseph Channel to visit the locks at Lake Superior or to cruise on Lake Superior.

Chart 2251.

Mile 114.0. Heading 221T from Thessalon will put you at the entrance to Potagannissing Bay at mile 128.0. .

Chart 14822.

Mile 128.0 Potagannissing Bay. Pass midway between Cherry Island and Hay Point to enter Potagannissing Bay. This bay offers hundreds of islands to explore and provides many fine anchorages. ou have just entered US waters. **Note -** You must clear customs and immigration at your first landfall in the US. With new security requirements it will be necessary to stop in person at a customs station and show documentation. Drummond Island provides the only on-site Customs Office in the area. Stop at Drummond Island Yacht Haven (906-493-5232,G,D,P) to clear customs. This is the point where you will require your US User Fee Decal that I reminded you to get back on page 5. Grocery and post office within 0.5 miles.

One popular and protected anchorage in Potagannissing Bay is Harbor Island. About 1.5 miles north of Drummond Island Yacht Haven, Harbor Island offers two protected anchorages. Approach Harbor Island from the SW and there is an anchorage in the SW corner of the island protected on three sides that provides good protection for deep draft vessels in 10-12'. Or, you can follow the channel a short way into the inner harbor (depending on your draft) for excellent protection in all winds and anchor in soft mud in 6-8'. Waters shoal as you head further into the inner harbor. (#24)

Mile 138.0, De Tour Village. There is NO good anchorage close to De Tour Village. There is an inexpensive protected marina there that provides a good place to take on fuel and stock up before your journey west. Within four blocks of the marina there is a grocery store, hardware, Laundromat, post office, bank (where you can change that pesky Canadian money), restaurants and a bakery.

Do Not Use For Navigation

Cruising The Trent-Severn Waterway, Georgian Bay, And North Channel
Chapter 10 – The North Channel

The DeTour Harbor Marina (906-297-5947,G,D,P) has transient space for more than 50 larger boats. 50A electric, showers and E-mail hookup.

De Tour Village ends any trip up the North Channel. In the next chapter we will cover the harbors on the more exposed northern end of Lake Huron leading to the Straits of Mackinac and Lake Michigan.

DeTour Reef Light

Cruising The Trent Severn Waterway, Georgian Bay, And North Channel

Chapter 11
Northern Lake Huron

For most cruisers departing De Tour Village means heading west for Lake Michigan via the Straits of Mackinac. The natural stop in route is Mackinac Island. However, the harbor at Mackinac Island can be very rough with all the ferry traffic and uncomfortable in the best of times. Instead many boaters are now stopping at one of the alternative harbors and taking the ferry to visit Mackinac Island. It is a little more expensive that way, but Mackinac Island should not be missed and you may be more comfortable staying in St Ignace or Mackinaw City. All the possible stops covered in this chapter are within 50 miles of De Tour Village, and thus, for most boaters within a days run.

This chapter covers cruising the upper waters of Lake Huron near the Straits of Mackinac. (Mackinac is pronounced "mack-i-naw") It doesn't matter if is Mackinaw City, Old Mackinac Point, or Mackinac Island. It is pronounced like the wool coat, mackinaw. It comes from the word Michilimackinac, a French word for the area used by the Ojibway Indians. "Michili" means "Giant" and "Mackinac" means "Turtle". Some believe the name comes from the fact that Mackinac Island looks like a giant turtle. But, this is doubtful. After all, 200 years ago, how could the Indians get an overhead view of the island and have any idea of what it looks like? The true origins of the word are lost in antiquity, but you will hear a wide variety of stores about the name and it's origin while in the area. Just pronounce it correctly, or you may as well wear a large sign hanging from a rope around your neck that says, "I'm not from here, help me I'm lost!"

Most of the area around Mackinac Island is a tourist destination, which is extremely popular in the summer months. While Mackinac Island is a must stop, either on your own boat or by ferry, there are also other places well worth visiting while in the area. Since there is no "one route", this chapter of the book will be different than all the rest. It will not be presented "by the mile". Instead all of the interesting

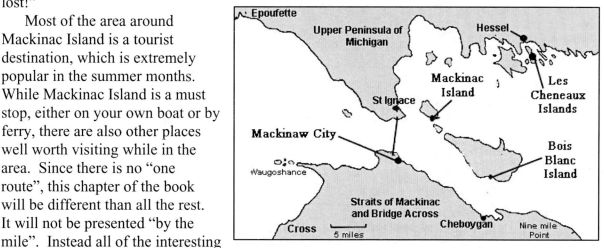

harbors will be presented with their location, places to anchor or tie up at marinas, and highlights and shopping ashore. The NOAA Charts used are 14881 and 14885.

The harbors presented in the rest of this chapter are given in a counterclockwise direction starting at De Tour Village and ending at Cheboygan, MI as shown on the figure above.

Do Not Use For Navigation

Cruising the Trent-Severn Waterway, Georgian Bay and North Channel
Chapter 11 – Northern Lake Huron

Les Cheneaux Islands

Les Cheneaux Islands are located along the northwest shore of Lake Huron about 20 miles west of De Tour Village or 15 miles east of Mackinac Island. Or, roughly half way between De Tour Village and Mackinac Island. This group of islands provides an excellent place to explore, enjoy protected sailing and anchor out. There are a couple of small villages in the area of more than 100 islands where you can get supplies. A quick glance at the charts will show that there are several channels where you can enter the more protected areas of this group of islands. However, from the east I recommend the main channel at N45° 56.9 and W84° 17.1 as shown on page 12 at buoy G1 just off the tip of Government Island.

Keep your greens on port (red right returning) as you work your way up the deep channel east of Government Island towards the village of Cedarville. In route to Cedarville you pass one of the best anchorages in this island group in Government Bay. The water is clear in Les Cheneaux Islands and you should be able to see the bottom at 10'. Thus, navigation at slow speeds with someone on the bow opens up a lot of possible anchorages in this area, besides Government Bay.

If you trace a zigzag line north around the northern end of La Salle Island, back to the south on the west side and then north again around Connors Point you will approach Mackinac Bay. From Mackinac Bay another zig and zag west takes you to Hessel at the head of Marquette Bay, and the west most entrance of the Les Cheneaux Islands. Following this route you will find a number of good anchorages and I will point out one or two for you. The bottom is generally good holding in mud throughout this area. Expect a lot of small craft traffic during the day, particularly on weekends and holidays. This traffic dies down at night.

Some boaters refer to Les Cheneaux Islands as "the snows". Cheneaux is the French translation of the Indian word for "channels". You will hear this area called all three; the snows, the channels or Les Cheneaux. Most of the shoreline is privately owned and not available for landing. The exception is Government Island, which is public land and provides beaches and picnic areas. The rest of the land in Les Cheneaux is lightly settled and quiet peaceful anchorages abound.

From the east the first village you come to is Cedarville north of La Salle Island. Cedarville does not provide any thing but a day anchorage close by. Cedarville Marine (906-484-2815,G,D,P) is your best bet for overnight dockage. In Cedarville you will find restaurants, small shops, post office and an ice cream shop. For serious shopping you will find grocery, beer and liquor, hardware, pharmacy, and Laundromat between 1 and 1.3 miles from the marina.

Continuing toward the west from Cedarville, the red markers are now on your port (red right returning) as you are leaving Cedarville and headed for open water. In route to Hessel, you will find a good anchorage in the south end of Muscallonge Bay and another one at the southeast end of Hessel Bay.

At the north end of Hessel Bay is the village of Hessel. Again the only anchorage in this area would be considered a day stop in good weather. You will frequently see boats at anchor off Cube Point to the south of Hessel. The Clark Township Public Dock (906-484-3917,P) provides transient space. In Hessel you are closer to shopping with a small grocery near the marina and restaurants. Hessel celebrates wooden boats the second Saturday in August and the harbor is a mad house with virtually no dockage available.

From Hessel it is only about 15 miles to Mackinac Island, but boaters frequently anchor in either Wilderness Bay or Maquette Bay as they depart Hessel south bound. Both provide good

Do Not Use For Navigation
Page - 72

Cruising the Trent-Severn Waterway, Georgian Bay and North Channel
Chapter 11 – Northern Lake Huron

protection in the prevailing SW winds, but are to be avoided in unsettled weather or when the winds are coming from the NW.

Saint Ignace

19 miles SW of Hessel and 6 miles west of Mackinac Island harbor is best known as a ferry landing for Mackinac Island at the northern end of the Mackinac Bridge. The one marina in Saint Ignace is located at N45° 52 and W84° 43. It is possible to anchor off Saint Ignace, but the large wakes of the many ferries will make your anchorage uncomfortable. The marina is better protected with a large breakwater.

The St. Ignace Municipal Marina (906-643-8131,G,D,P) has 130 slips and provides transient space for about 90 boats. In the small village you will find a Glen's Market, hardware store, library, Laundromat, pharmacy, and restaurants. All are on or near State Street, the main drag.

If time permits visit the Marquette Mission Park and Museum, Fort Debaude Museum, Michilimackinac Historical Society Museum, or the Father Marquette National Memorial and Museum. All relate to the early French and Indian history of this area and are very educational. To visit the present day Indians of the area, take a taxi to the Kewadin Casino (just kidding about the Indians) and throw some of your extra money away.

Mackinac Island

In the center of this cruising area is Mackinac Island, the gold at the end of the rainbow. This island is known by nearly everyone that stops here, long before they arrive. It has been forever imbedded in our memories by book, song and movie. Who doesn't remember Christopher Reeve in Somewhere in Time. The scenes on the porch of the Grand Hotel are etched in our memories. However, today if you want to simply walk on that porch, it will be $7 please. Yes, Mackinac Island is historic, beautiful, quaint and very expensive.

The entrance to the harbor at the south end of Mackinac Island is at N43° 50.6 and W84° 36.9. Virtually all the major tourist attractions are close to this harbor, but the large island does offer many other places to visit. Inside the harbor there is only one marina. The Mackinac Island Municipal Harbor (906-847-3561,P) is the only game in town and very, very busy. When you are in sight of the marina call on VHF-14 or by phone to arrange for a slip assignment. During normal periods you will be placed on a waiting list. You cannot be put on the list until the dockmaster sees your vessel, so don't bother trying. There is a four-day maximum stay in the marina and then you must vacate the marina. This will barely give you time to see and do all that there is available on this island. Many vessels anchor just to the east inside the harbor entrance, while waiting for a slip assignment. Some simply stay on the hook for their entire visit. Holding is not good in this area. Many boats have dragged and gone ashore in the harbor area.

The harbor is very busy with ferries coming and going at all hours. Do not bother to complain about the ferryboat wake. No one ashore cares. The ferries are the bread and butter lifeline of this island and speed is all they care about. Obviously the best slip assignment is on the inside, but beggars cannot be choosers.

Ashore automobiles are not permitted and transportation is by horse and buggy or bicycle. While the very touristy village is spread out on the hillside in front of the marina, the heaviest concentration is right along the waterfront. Dominating the hillside is Fort Mackinac. A long walk up the hill and you can spend the better part of a day exploring this interesting historical site.

In town the shops are dominated by what you would expect in a tourist Mecca. There are many restaurants and gift shops. There is a small food market, bank, pharmacy, etc. But don't expect much here except places for tourists. Take a bicycle tour, a horse carriage tour, or a walking tour. Pick up a current Mackinac Island map from nearly any shop and explore to your hearts content. Explore Fort Mackinac or just enjoy the ambience of the rich homes in the area. Be sure to try Mackinac Island Fudge. This is a stop you won't soon forget and one you will treasure for the rest of your life.

Mackinaw City

On the south side of the Straits of Mackinac where the Mackinac Bridge comes ashore is Mackinaw City. (At least they spell it correctly) The harbor consists mainly of the Mackinaw City Municipal Marina (616-436-5269,G,D,P) behind a well-constructed breakwater. Inside the basin there is room for about 60 boats. Shepler's Marine (231-436-7287) operates a ships store and full service yard adjacent to the Municipal Marina. This is a busy harbor and during the period of the Great Lake Sailboat races in July may be full. The entrance is at N45° 46.9 and W84° 43.25.

The Grand Hotel on Mackinac Island

Mackinaw City is probably the best choice of a place to leave your boat and take the ferry to Mackinac Island. The basin is better protected than St. Ignace. The ferry is a two-block walk to the south from the marina.

It is possible to anchor off Mackinaw City, and dinghy ashore, but it is not recommended due to the heavy boat wakes from all the ferry traffic.

Mackinaw City has had an extensive face lift in recent years. You can get around by trolley or simply walk to more than 100 shops and restaurants in the immediate area of the marina. Within a few blocks you will find liquor, bakery, drug store, movie complex, Laundromat, many gift shops, live performance theater, and a shopping mall called Mackinaw Crossings.

There are two major tourist attractions at Mackinaw City. Fort Michilimackinac and the Mackinac Bridge. You will probably go under the bridge during your travels and see as much of it as you care to. However, if time permits take a walk to Colonial Michilimackinac State Park and the remains of a fort by the same name. A completely restored colonial village awaits your arrival, which is sure to enthrall you with its accuracy. Downtown you will also find the Mackinac Bridge Museum with lots of interesting information on this famous bridge.

Cruising the Trent-Severn Waterway, Georgian Bay and North Channel
Chapter 11 – Northern Lake Huron

Bois Blanc Island

South of Mackinac Island is the much larger Bois Blanc Island. Bois Blanc is French for White Wood, for the white birch, which used to dominate the island. Today Bois Blanc Island is nearly uninhabited, but does provide dockage and a place to stop at a state park. Located on the south side of the island the ferry landing and Bois Blanc Island State Dock are at N45º 43.60 and W84º 27.00.

A "J" shaped breakwater hooked to the east forms the harbor. Just inside the end of the breakwater on the west are the slips for the park dockage. There is room for about 8 boats. A short way in on the breakwater is the ferry dock, which provides transportation to and from the island for the few residents.

There is not much in the way of shopping on Bois Blanc Island. It is a peaceful almost serene location where you can walk or bicycle for miles. There is a grocery store about 0.2 miles west of the harbor with limited supplies. A couple small restaurants are available on the island, but more than 1-mile walk from the harbor. Bois Blanc Island is not the place to stop to re-provision your ships stores, but rather to re-provision your soul. Take a couple days here to relax and commune with nature.

Cheboygan

Cheboygan lies on the southern shore of the South Channel due south of Bois Blanc Island. The entrance buoy, R2, is at N45º 40.0 and W84º 4. From this buoy follow the well-marked and deep channel SW into Cheboygan. Favor the red side all the way in to the first bridge.

Just inside the entrance jetty on the west side is a basin with the Cheboygan County Marina (231-627-4944,G,D,P) and transient space. This marina is a little removed from the town of Cheboygan and boaters may prefer the marinas available closer to town. Proceed up the Cheboygan River and on the east bank just before the bascule bridge is Walstrom Marine (231-627-6681,P). Walstrom Marine is primarily a boat yard, but does have alongside dockage with 30A electric and a restaurant. Adjacent to the Walstrom Marine is the USCGC Mackinaw, now a museum and open to the public.

Unfortunately there are no anchoring possibilities in Cheboygan. The first possibility is well past the end of the Cheboygan River and on the Inland Waterway.

More marina facilities are just past the State Street Bascule Bridge. This bridge has 9' clearance when down and responds to VHF-16. It opens every 30 minutes starting at 15 minutes after the hour during summer months.

Just past the bridge on the west shore is the Cheboygan Public dock with transient space, 30A electric, restrooms and showers. This stop is much closer to town. A little further in on the west side also is the Anchor-In Marina (231-627-4620,G,P) with transient space.

There is a small convenience store 2 blocks south on Main Street as well as the usual restaurants and small shops in the immediate area of the public docks. However, for real grocery shopping ask for directions to one of two Grocery stores, both about a 1-mile walk. In town you will find a taxi service and a restored opera house where musical performances are presented on occasion.

Cheboygan is best known to boaters today for providing access to the Inland Waterway. This waterway uses canals and locks to connect Cheboygan thru a series of lakes almost to the shores of Lake Michigan. If you can carry your boat the last 10 miles, you could go from Cheboygan to

Cruising the Trent-Severn Waterway, Georgian Bay and North Channel
Chapter 11 – Northern Lake Huron

Lake Michigan and not go thru the Straits of Mackinac. Indians and frontiersman used to portage this stretch with their canoes. To explore the Inland Waterway, your vessel must have a draft of 4' or less and an air clearance of 16' or less. If your vessel meets these requirements, feel free to take a few days to a week to explore the very narrow and twisty Inland Waterway about 40 miles to Crooked Lake. Expect a lot of small boat company along the way and remember that the locks and waterway begin to close for the season in September. There is a small fee for use of the lock. You will need the NOAA chart 14886 for this waterway.

If you need to leave your boat for a short period, Cheboygan makes a lot of sense as a safe harbor where you could leave it. There is no major airport there, but you can rent cars nearby. Cheboygan offers the best-protected harbor near the Straits of Mackinac where one might leave a boat.

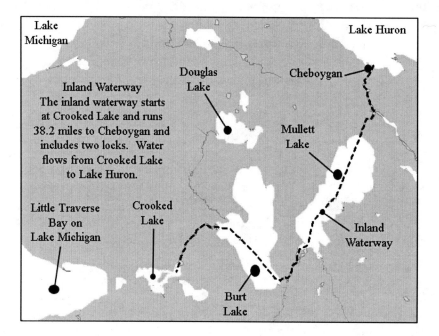

Do Not Use For Navigation

Appendix 1
Charts and Reference Books

Required charts for the Trent-Severn Waterway:
Canadian Hydrographic Chart 2021 ($28), 2022 ($23), 2023 ($23), 2024 ($33), 2025 ($23), 2028 ($23), and 2029 ($18). Prices in Canadian dollars.

Required charts for the Georgian Bay and North Channel:
Canadian Hydrographic Chart 2202 ($33), 2203 ($23), 2204 ($28), 2245 ($20), 2251 ($20), 2257 ($20), 2259 ($20), 2299 ($20). Prices in Canadian dollars.

NOAA charts 14881 ($21.95), 14882 ($21.95). Prices in U.S. dollars.

Other Resources:

Richardson's Chartbook & Cruising Guide, Lake Huron (including Georgian Bay & the North Channel).

Waterway Guide, Great Lakes 2008 Edition.

Cruising The Trent-Severn Canal, Georgian Bay, And North Channel

Appendix 2
Hours of Operation and Fees

Hours of Operation:

May 16 – June 19, 2008

Monday to Thursday – Open 9:00 – Last Lockage 4:00
Friday to Sunday – Open 9:00 – Last Lockage 7:00
Victoria Day – Open 9:00 – Last Lockage 7:00

June 20 – September 1, 2008

All days – Open 8:30 – Last Lockage 7:00

September 2 – October 15, 2007

Monday to Friday – Open 9:00 – Last Lockage 3:30
Saturday and Sunday - Open 9:00 – Last Lockage 5:30
Thanksgiving Day – Open 9:00 – Last Lockage 5:30

At most locks, vessels must arrive at or before the last lockage time.
At locks 11/12, 16/17, 20 and 21, vessels must arrive at least 15 minutes before the last lockage.
At swing bridges, the last bridge swing will be 20 minutes after the last lockage time.

Lockage Permits:

Single Lock and Return - $0.90/ft.
Single Day - $1.60/ft.
Transit one-way - $4.45/ft.
Six Day - $4.85/ft.
Seasonal - $8.80/ft.

Mooring Rates:

Overnight - $0.90/ft.
Seasonal Overnight - $9.80/ft.

Additional information may be obtained by visiting www.trentsevern.com/locks/fees.cfm
Fees are in Canadian dollars.

Cruising The Trent-Severn Canal, Georgian Bay, And North Channel

Appendix 3
Contributors

The following individuals contributed to material in this book. Their information is acknowledged and gratefully appreciated. Those that wish to contribute updates, corrections or additions should email them to skipperbob@att.net.

Don and Jean Halsell, *Wanderlust II*
Jim and Mary Ann Stimpson, *Tug Jimary*
Ron Solis
Don and Ruth Kalen, *Odyssey*
Doug Hobson and Elaine Trefler, *Bravo*
Brenda Otto, Campbellford Chamber of Commerce
Roger and Bonnie Ford, *Kokomo*
Barbara and Norman Hewton, *Beta Omega*
Steve Kromer, AGLCA
Fred and Donna Hammond, *Love Story*
John Slattery, *Irish Rover*
Fran and Steve Rice, *Spirit Chaser*
Denny Gustafson, *Temptress*
Jim Wooli
Bob and Ching, *Alligator*
Ken and Linda Croall, *Day Dreamer*
Alan Lloyd
Phil and Barney, *Apolonia*
Robin and Roger, *Sea Robbin*
Bob and Carol Kunath, *Sans Souci*
Tom and Pam Lazio, *Tom Boy*
Marcia and Jay Bench, *Livin' Easy*
Sal and Frank Bulkley, *Fine Romance*
Harold and Dee Rudd, *Lady Dee*
Ted and Audrey Stehle, *Good Times*
Norma Young, The North Channel Yacht Club

Cruising the Trent-Severn Canal, Georgian Bay and North Channel

Index

Admiral's Marina, 55
Anchor Island, 67
Anchor-In Marina, 75
Annual Mooring Pass, 20
Appendix 1, 77
Appendix 2, 78
Arrival in Canada, 12
Ashburnham, 31
Audrey's Cove Marina, 30
Baie Fine, 64
Balsam Lake, 39
Batawa, 23
Bay Moorings YC, 54
Bay Port Yachting, 53
Bayfield Harbour, 60
Beacon Bay Marina, 54
Beausoleil Island, 56
Beaverton Harbour, 42
Beaverton Yacht Club, 42
Beer Store, 13
Benjamin Islands, 67
Big Chute Marina, 47
Big Chute, 46
Big Sound Marina, 58
Birch Point Marina, 37
Blind River Marina, 68
Blind River, 68
Blue Beacon Marina, 43
Blue Hole, 24
Blue Line, 18
Bobcaygeon, 37
Bois Blanc Island, 75
Bolsover, 41
Bone Island, 56
Boyle Marine, 66
Bridal Veil Falls, 67
Brules Point, 72
Buckhorn Yacht Harbour, 36
Buckhorn, 36
Buoy BY, 53
Burleigh Falls, 35
Burnt Island, 62
Bush's Boat Livery, 48
Campbellford, 26
Canal fees,19
CanPass, 8
Carveth's Marina, 35

Cash, 9
CC Kennedy Co, 59
Cedar Cove Resort, 30
Cedarville Marine, 72
Cedarville, 72
Centre Point Marina, 37
Channels, 72
Chapter 1, 6
Chapter 2, 14
Chapter 3, 17
Chapter 4, 22
Chapter 5, 29
Chapter 6, 34
Chapter 7, 39
Chapter 8, 45
Chapter 9, 50
Chapter 10, 63
Chapter 11, 71
Cheboygan Marina, 75
Cheboygan Public Dock, 75
Cheboygan, 75
Chocolate Factory, 26
Cigarette Limits, 9
Clapperton Island, 66
Clark Township Dock, 72
Clear Lake, 35
Coboconk, 39
Collins Inlet, 61, 62
Colonial Michilimackinac, 74
Contributors, 11, 79
Couchiching, 45
Covered Portage Cove, 64
Crabby Indian, 62
Croker Island, 67
Crowe Bay, 26
Cube Point, 73
Customs, 7
De Tour Village, 69
Dead Island, 61
Deep Bay, 46
Delawana Inn Resort, 55
Discovery Harbour, 53
Doral Marine Resort, 53
Douro, 32
Dunroe Island, 57
Dundas Street Bridge, 22
Dutch Marine, 33

Eagle Island, 67
East Rous Island, 66
Electrical, 10
Entry Documentation, 7
Exchanging money, 9
FCC, 11
Fenelon Falls Marina, 38
Fenelon Falls, 38
Fishing, 10
Five Mile Bay, 57
Form I-68, 7
Fort Mackinac, 73
Fox Island, 36
Frankford, 24
Frazer Bay Hill, 65
Frying Pan Bay, 55
Fryingpan Island, 56
Gamebridge, 41
Gateway Marine, 64
Georgian Bay, 50
Glen Miller, 21
Glen Ross, 22
Gloucester Pool, 44
Goat Island, 66
Golden Beach Resort, 29
Gordon Yacht Harbour, 37
Gore's Landing Marina, 30
Grand Hotel, 74
Great La Cloche Island, 66
GST, 10
Guard Gate, 29
Gun Barrel, 61
Gun, 11
Haig's Reach, 25
Handgun, 11
Hangdog Marina, 60
Harbour View Marina, 65
Hardy Island, 27
Harwood Bridge, 30
Harwood, 30
Hastings Village Marina, 28
Hastings, 28, 29
Healey Falls, 27
Hells Gate, 35
Herbert Fisheries, 60
Hessel Bay, 72
Hessel, 72

Page - 80

Cruising the Trent-Severn Canal, Georgian Bay and North Channel
Index

Highest point, 39
Hindson Marine, 54
History, 14
Holding tank, 10
Hole in the Wall Bridge, 40
Honey Harbour, 54
Hot Knots Marina, 43
I-68, 7
Indian Harbour, 56
Inland Waterway, 76
Jack Island, 59
Jackson Island, 68
Jett Island, 24
John Island, 68
Kagawong, 66
Kawartha Lakes, 34
Kawartha Park Marina, 35
Killarney Mountain Lodge, 64
Killarney, 64
Kineras Bay, 54
Kirkfield Lift Lock, 40
Kirkfield, 40
Lagoon City Marina, 42
Lake Couchiching, 43
Lake levels, 52
Lake Simcoe, 42
Lakefield Marina, 34
Lakefield, 32, 33
Lang's Resort, 29
Largest vessel, 33
Lauderdale Point Marina, 45
LDBO, 10
LeBlan's Sans Souci, 56
Les Cheneaux Islands, 72
Little Chute, 48
Little Current, 65
Little Detroit Strait, 67
Lock 1, 22
Lock 2, 23
Lock 3, 23
Lock 4, 23
Lock 5, 23
Lock 6, 24
Lock 7, 24
Lock 8, 24
Lock 9, 25
Lock 10, 25
Lock 11, 25

Lock 12, 25
Lock 13, 26
Lock 14, 26
Lock 15, 27
Lock 16, 27
Lock 17, 27
Lock 18, 28
Lock 19, 30
Lock 20, 31
Lock 21, 32
Lock 22, 32
Lock 23, 32
Lock 24, 32
Lock 25, 32
Lock 26, 32
Lock 27, 34
Lock 28, 35
Lock 29, 35
Lock 30, 35
Lock 31, 36
Lock 32, 37
Lock 34, 38
Lock 35, 38
Lock 36, 40
Lock 37, 41
Lock 38, 41
Lock 39, 41
Lock 40, 41
Lock 41, 41
Lock 42, 45
Lock 43, 46
Lock 44, 46
Lock 45, 48
Locking pass, 17
Lost Channel, 46
Lovesick, 35
Mackinac Bridge, 74
Mackinac Island Fudge, 74
Mackinac Island Harbor, 73
Mackinac Island, 73
Mackinaw City Marina, 74
Mackinaw City, 74
MacMillian's, 26
Mafor, 51
Maria Street Bridge, 31
Marina del Rey, 42
Mariner's Point Marina, 43
Mariposa Beach, 40

Markers change sides, 40
Marquette Bay, 72
Mars Marina, 36
Mary Ann Cove, 65
McBean Channel, 64
McCrackens, Landing, 35
McDonalds Cut, 46
McGregor Marina, 43
McPhee Bay, 42
McRae Point Park, 42
Meyers, 25
Midland Harbour, 53
Midland Marina, 53
Midland, 53
Military Museum, 26
Mitchell Lake, 39
Moon Bay, 56
Mooring Pass, 20
MSD I, 10
MSD III, 10
Muscallonge Bay, 69
Musquash Channel, 56
Narrows Island, 559
Narrows, 43, 48
Nassau Mills, 32
Navigation caution, 11
Norgate Rocks, 60
North Channel, 61
North Channel Yacht Club, 68
Northern Lake Huron, 67
Northern Marina, 67
Number of locks, 17
O'Dannel Point, 56
O'Hara Point Marina, 48
Old Mill Park, 26
Orillia, 43
Orillia Island, 43
Otonabee River, 30
Otonabee, 30
Paragon Marina, 54
Parry Sound Marine, 58
Parry Sound, 57
Payne Marine, 59
Penetanguishene, 53
Percy Reach, 24
Peterborough Marina, 31
Peterborough, 31
Pets, 10

Cruising the Trent-Severn Canal, Georgian Bay and North Channel
Index

Picnic Island resort, 54
Pier 99 Marina, 58
Pigeon Lake, 37
Plank Road Cottages, 30
Point Au Baril, 59
Point Pleasant Marina, 58
Port of Call Marina, 41
Port Rawson, 56
Port Severn, 48. 52
Portage, 41
Potagannissing Bay, 69
Provisions, 9
Rabies, 10
Radio License, 11
Railway Lock, 47
Ranney Falls, 25
Reach Harbour Marine, 36
Reach Harbour, 36
Red Right Returning, 19
Redner Bay, 57
Regatta Bay, 53
Required charts, 73
Rice Lake, 29
ROC, 11
Rogers island, 61
Rogue's Marina, 64
Rose Point RR Bridge, 53
Rosedale Marina, 38
Rosedale, 38
Saint Ignace, 73
Sandy Bay, 61
Sanford island, 68
Sawyer Creek, 32
Scott Mills, 30
Seasonal Locking Pass, 19
Secretary island, 63
Severn Boat Haven, 48
Severn Falls, 46
Severn Marina, 48
Severn River, 48
Shawanaga Inlet, 59
Sir John Simcoe, 39
Small Craft Channel, 52
Snows, 72
Snug Harbor, 58, 64
Sources of publications, 2

South Bay, 55
South Bay Cover Marina, 55
South Channel, 57
Spanish Marina, 68
Spanish, 68
Speed limit, 18
Spider Bay Marina, 66
Spider Bay, 56
Sportsman's Inn, 64
St. Amant's Marina, 60
St. Ignace Public Dock, 73
Starport Landing, 42
Stay on lock wall, 20
Steam Mill Island, 28
Stony Lake, 35
Straits of Mackinac, 71
Sturgeon Bay, 66
Sturgeon Lake, 37
Sunset Cove Marina, 41
Swift rapids, 46
Sydney, 23
Table of Contents, 5
Talbot River, 39
Talbot, 41
Thessalon Marina, 69
Thessalon, 68
The Sound Boatworks, 58
Thompson Marine, 60
Thorah, 41
Tie Island, 61
Trent Canal, 39
Trent River, 27, 45
Trent, 23
Trenton River, 12
Trenton, 12
Trent-Severn History, 14
Trent-Severn Information, 6
Trent-Severn Map, 6, 17
Turner's Service Station, 26
Twelve Mile Bay, 56
Twin Cedar Cottages, 29
Tying up in lock, 17
User Decal, 8
Viamede Resort, 35
Walstrom Marina, 75
Warsaw Road Bridge, 32

Water levels, 52
Weapons, 11
Weather forecast, 51
Whites Falls Marina, 48
Wilderness Bay, 72
Wright's Marina, 60
Young's Point Marina, 34
Young's Point, 34